P9-DHJ-235

THE SUPER SCRAP-CRAFT BOOK

Quick and Easy Projects with a Great Look

THE SUPER SCRAP-CRAFT BOOK

Quick and Easy Projects with a Great Look

by

*Artis Aleene Eckstein, Heidi Borchers,
and Tiffany Windsor*

Photographs by Darryl Antrim

NAL BOOKS

NEW AMERICAN LIBRARY

TIMES MIRROR

NEW YORK AND SCARBOROUGH, ONTARIO

AN ANDIRON PRESS BOOK

Copyright © 1983 by Artis Aleene Eckstein,
Heidi Hall Borchers, and Tiffany Michele Windsor

All rights reserved

For information address The New American Library, Inc.

Published simultaneously in Canada by
The New American Library of Canada Limited

NAL BOOKS TRADEMARK REG. U.S. PAT. OFF. AND FOREIGN COUNTRIES
REGISTERED TRADEMARK—MARCA REGISTRADA
HECHO EN HARRISONBURG, VA., U.S.A.

SIGNET, SIGNET CLASSICS, MENTOR, PLUME, MERIDIAN and
NAL BOOKS are published *in the United States* by
The New American Library, Inc.,
1633 Broadway, New York, New York 10019,
in Canada by The New American Library of Canada Limited,
81 Mack Avenue, Scarborough, Ontario M1L 1M8

Library of Congress Cataloging in Publication Data

Eckstein, Artis Aleene.
   The super scrap-craft book.

Includes index.
   1. Handicraft.   2. Waste products.   3. Recycling
(Waste, etc.) I. Borchers, Heidi. II. Windsor,
Tiffany.   III. Title.
TT157.E36   1983   745.58′4   82-24875
ISBN 0-453-00439-3

Designed by Julian Hamer

First Printing, June, 1983

1   2   3   4   5   6   7   8   9

PRINTED IN THE UNITED STATES OF AMERICA

Dedicated to our families, who have spent their lives involved in *our* arts and crafts, supporting us in our activities, collecting junk for our projects, and never complaining when vacations turned into craft shows and tours.

Contents

Introduction

The idea behind this book is that you use what you have available. Fabric remnants, assorted buttons, beads, and bows left from needlework projects; empty plastic bottles, foil trays, egg cartons, and brown paper bags; found objects like driftwood, shells, and pinecones: these are a scrap-crafter's stock, just as substituting or "making do" is a scrap-crafter's skill. If the lace edging or braid tucked away in the bedroom drawer is ⅜-inch instead of ¼-inch, if the fabric remnant is a print instead of a solid, use it: we won't tell if you don't.

Most of us are busy these days, so we just don't have time for painstakingly slow projects. This book focuses on designs that usually can be made in one sitting. Although requiring only minimum skills, it has an abundance of eye-catchers and something for every taste. It will appeal to anyone interested in producing salable and makable gifts and ornaments with a great look (bazaar chairmen, please note). The chapter on super-simple projects will provide many happy—and educational hours—for children, as they learn to see beauty and function even in ordinary household objects ready for the trash pile (teachers and youth leaders, please note).

Scrap-crafters are a special kind of people. They believe in the maxim "Waste not, want not," and find deep satisfaction in making an elegant little something from nothing; saving money by doing so may be beside the point for them. But if you're budget-conscious, this book will be right for you, because it shows you how to create inexpensive home ornaments, jewelry, and handmade (and therefore much appreciated) gifts.

Now it's time for you to start. We hope you and your family will have many happy hours and super-satisfaction as you craft your way through these pages.

HOW TO USE THE PATTERNS

The projects are actual-size except those with grids; these patterns will be actual size when drawn to the scale indicated below each pattern. *To enlarge patterns,* you will need a sharp pencil, ruler, and paper. To make graph, mark a sheet of paper with dots at the intervals called for in each pattern. For instance, if the pattern is 1 square = $\frac{5}{16}$ inch, mark dots $\frac{5}{16}$ of an inch apart horizontally and vertically on your paper. With your ruler, join these dots to make $\frac{5}{16}$-inch squares. Count squares on your graph paper to make sure it has the same number of horizontal and vertical squares as on the pattern. If a larger graph is needed, piece together sheets of paper. Enlarge the design by copying the pattern one square at a time onto the graph paper you've created. Don't worry if you're not artistically inclined and your patterns are not exact. Use them as guides and have fun! Then follow one of these steps.

1. trace the actual-size pattern directly on the material called for in the individual project;
2. or glue the actual-size pattern to lightweight cardboard and cut around the outline. Trace the outline onto the material as required by the design and continue as indicated. The cardboard template is durable and can be easily duplicated if you wish to make more than one of a given item. You can also pin or clip the template to several layers of thin papers, fabric, etc., enabling you to cut through them simultaneously.

To use patterns same size, copy them freehand onto the material called for in the individual project, or trace them as suggested in steps 1 or 2 above.

CHAPTER ONE

Creating with Natural Materials

Perhaps because our environment is so threatened these days, most of us have an extraordinary instinct to preserve and cherish the materials provided in such abundance by a prodigal Nature. In this chapter we focus on shells, pods, cones, flowers, leaves, seeds, and even husks, and we hope that you will like the results as much as we do. Please remember that no two "naturals" are ever exactly alike, so don't try for an exact replica of any of our designs. Substitution is the key to creativity.

Seashell Angel

Materials:

30" white 2-ply yarn, strung on
   needle, for hair
1 wooden bead ⅝" diameter,
   painted flesh-color, for head
White tacky glue
Permanent fine-line black
   marking pen
3" piece 22-gauge wire
2" seashell for body (see note)
Hot glue
5" x 5" piece embossed gold paper
   for wings
6" narrow ribbon for bow
6" gold cord for hanger

Instructions:

To make angel's hair, thread yarn
on needle through bead, leaving
approximately 1 inch of yarn at
end to hold on to. Bring needle
around and through bead in same
direction for about nine times,
until yarn covers almost two-
thirds of the bead. Cut yarn, leaving 2 inches on bead. Glue wire
into bead end opposite bun, and
use wire to hold on to bead while
making bun and face. *For bun,*
apply a small dab of tacky glue
around base of 2-inch end of yarn.
Starting from the center, coil
yarn around in a circle. Tuck end
of yarn under coil, securing with
a dab of tacky glue. Draw the
eyes, nose, and mouth onto the
bead head with marking pen, following photograph. Shape wire to
fit inside shell. Place hot glue at
base of head and all along wire to
secure head to shell. Cut wings
from gold paper, following pattern. Glue wings on back of angel.
Glue bow under neck. Glue a loop
of gold cord to head for hanger.
Note: Measure the shell lengthwise; if your shell is larger than,
say, 3 inches, increase the diameter of the bead to 1 inch.

DESIGNING WITH SHELLS

Hidden in rocks and tall
grasses that surround seas,
lakes, ponds, rivers, and bays
throughout the world, and on
sandy beaches too, of course,
one may find shells of infinite
variety and beauty. All shells
are useful in crafting, and they
are yours for the taking, but for
ecological reasons we suggest
that you take only empty or
dead shells, rather than those
housing live animals, and that
you take no more than you can
use.

Preparing Shells

The shells must be cleaned, so
wash them thoroughly in
warm, soapy water, then rinse
and dry. *To bleach shells,* soak
them in a solution of chlorine
bleach and water (about 2 tablespoons chlorine in a quart of
water). Remove the shells as
soon as they are clean and
fresh. Rinse again and dry.
You might like to enhance
their natural color and grain-
ing by rubbing them lightly
with baby oil. Shells with tarry
deposits should be discarded as
they are almost impossible to
clean.

WINGS

Seashell Country Maid

Materials:

60″ blond 2-ply yarn, strung on needle, for hair
1 wooden bead 1″ diameter, painted flesh-color, for head
White tacky glue
Permanent fine-line black and red marking pens
Toothpick, end blunted
Small amount pink acrylic paint for cheeks
2″ piece white chenille stem
Hot glue
3″ seashell for body
Fabric scraps for blouse, sleeves, and hat
Tiny dried or artificial flowers
Flesh-color felt scraps for hands
6″ gold cord for hanger (optional)

Instructions:

To make hair, thread yarn on needle through bead, leaving approximately 1 inch of yarn at end to hold on to. Bring needle around and through bead in same direction fourteen times, until yarn covers about two-thirds of bead. Cut yarn attached to needle about 2 inches from bead. *For braid,* cut 8-inch length of yarn. Fold in half, so that ends are even. Starting at bottom center of bead, insert even ends under closest strand and weave over second strand, repeating back and forth four times (see drawing). Tuck loose ends over at top and secure with a dab of glue to make bangs. Repeat with opposite side. Draw *eyes and mouth* on bead with black marking pen, *nose* with red pen. Form the heart-shaped *cheeks* by dabbing end of toothpick in pink paint and making two dots side by side. Then pull toothpick down from middle of each dot, forming two "teardrops" side by side, joining in middle to form heart. (First practice on a piece of paper.) Glue 2-inch chenille stem in hole in bead at the neck. Glue stem and head to shell with hot glue (curving stem to the

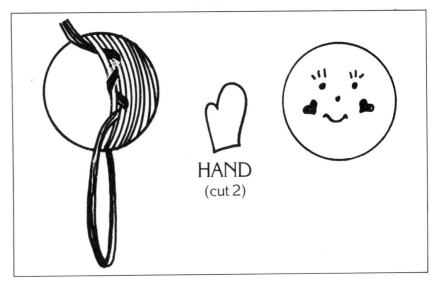

HAND
(cut 2)

shape of the shell before gluing down). *To make hat,* glue two thicknesses of fabric together with tacky glue. Cut a circle 2 inches in diameter with ¾-inch hole in center from the double thickness of fabric. Glue to top of head. Trim with flowers. The *sleeves* are made from scrap fabric cut ½ inch x 1¼ inches. Fold raw edges over and glue. Gather cuff ¼ inch from end by basting with needle and thread. Pull to gather and tie thread to hold gather. Glue sleeves in place, following photo. Fold sleeve excess to back of shell and glue in place. Cut two *hands* from felt, following pattern, and glue under each cuff. Glue flowers in between. Glue gold cord to head for hanger, if desired.

Seashell Bunny

Materials:

1 wooden bead 1″ diameter,
   painted white, for head
Permanent fine-line black
   marking pen
Wooden toothpick
Acrylic paint: red and pink
2 white chenille bumps for ears
1″ piece white chenille stem for
   neck
3″ seashell
Hot glue
6″ narrow ribbon for bow
3″ x 3″ white felt for hands
White tacky glue
White cotton pom-pom ½″
   diameter for tail
Cloth flower for trim
6″ gold cord for hanger (optional)

Instructions:

Draw *eyes and mouth* on wooden bead with marking pen following photograph. *For nose,* dab end of toothpick in red paint and dot onto bead. *For cheeks,* dot pink paint onto bead using photograph as guide. Make the *ears* by gluing the ends of the two chenille bumps in hole at top of bead. *For neck,* glue white chenille stem in hole at other end of bead, leaving ½ inch protruding from bottom of bead. Attach head to shell with hot glue, using chenille stem to help anchor head. Glue bow in place to cover stem at neck. Using pattern as guide, cut *hands and feet* from white felt. Glue to shell with white tacky glue. *For tail,* glue pom-pom on underside of shell ½ inch from shell edge, lining up between bunny's feet. Glue cloth flower in place between bunny's ears. Glue gold cord to head or shell for hanger, if desired.

HAND
(cut 2)

FOOT
(cut 2)

Pinecone Duck Decoy

Materials:

3 large pinecones, more if they are small
Wire cutters or scissors
9″ x 12″ felt for background
9″ x 12″ cardboard
White tacky glue
Ribbon bow for trim
Dried baby's-breath sprigs for trim
Frame (optional)

Instructions:

Pull scales from cones. If scales cannot be pulled off one by one, cut them off using wire cutters or kitchen shears. Select the widest scales at the bottom for best results. Cut rough edge of scale to a point. Cut one long scale for beak. Glue felt to cardboard for background. Draw outline of duck on board, following pattern. Arrange scales on the felt background before gluing; when design looks right, glue into place, overlapping them as shown in picture. Start from the back of design and work forward. Glue bow and baby's breath in place, using photo as guide. Frame, if desired.

CRAFTING WITH PINECONES AND PODS

Picking up pods and cones is fun for the entire family. You can find them in your backyard, on a walk around the neighborhood, or at an outing in the mountains, fields, or woods. There is a surprising variation in their forms, which adds to their versatility and design uses. Cones, for example, range in size from 2 inches to 12 inches long, and can be egg-shaped, cylindrical, pendulous, or round. Although cones from pines are the most common, other trees are coniferous too, so by all means collect what you find. Cone textures can represent the scales of a fish, the mane of a lion, the feathers of an owl, or the petals in a flower. Cut lengthwise or crosswise, or into individual scales, the cone can supply shingles for a doll house, or be made into a wreath.

Pods are equally versatile. In their simplest craft use, the pod (like the gourd) might by its own shape suggest a particular creature. With pipe cleaner feet, seeds for eyes, a dab of paint for a nose, the resemblance to an animal can be reinforced. Use your imagination. It's fun and educational to create your own aviary, aquarium, or zoo based on these free-for-the-taking materials. Articles for personal adornment and for home decoration are also shown in the designs which follow. So get out of doors and find those gifts from nature. (If this is impossible for you, cones and pods are also sold in craft stores.)

Instructions for preparing fresh cones and pods for use appear on page 8.

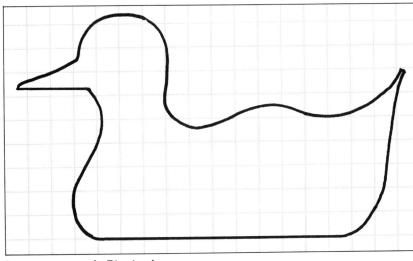

1 square equals 7/16 inch

Pinecone Parrot

HOW TO PREPARE CONES AND PODS

Select cones and pods while they are firm and fresh, before they have weathered. Pick them in all stages, from unripe (tightly closed) to mature (scales separated).

To clean the cones and pods, wash them quickly in water, then dry in a warm dry place (on a cookie sheet in a very slow oven, 150–175° F, is ideal). When they are totally free of moisture, store them in a large, covered container such as a box, large wide-mouthed jar, plastic container, etc. Add a few spoonfuls of borax to keep out mold and insects.

If the pinecones are sticky, you may have to bake them in a slow oven or put them in the sun until the pitch softens. Then scrub with a stiff brush or clean in turpentine or mineral spirits (following the usual precautions for flammable materials). Let dry thoroughly before you use or store them.

Dried cones and pods, nuts too, may be used in their natural color, or gilded, shellacked, lacquered, sprayed with clear plastic, varnished, bleached by the sun (turning them for even fading), or painted. The choice is yours.

To cut cones, use wire cutters or tin snips; twist off individual scales with a pair of long-nosed pliers.

Materials:

Pinecones
Wire cutters or scissors
9″ x 12″ felt for background
9″ x 12″ cardboard
White tacky glue
Small branch or twig (we've used a eucalyptus branch with pods)
Dried flowers for trim
Frame (optional)

Instructions:

Cut the wide scales from the bottom of the pinecone using wire cutters or scissors, and shape them to a point. Glue felt to cardboard for background. Draw outline of parrot on cardboard, following pattern. Arrange pinecone pieces and branch on outlined figure or felt before gluing them in. Glue branch on first, then glue upper portion of body, working downward. Reverse the petal shapes to create contrast in "feathers." Tail feathers are formed by working from the bottom of the tail upward toward the body. Glue strips of dried flowers onto branch, using photo as guide. Frame, if desired.

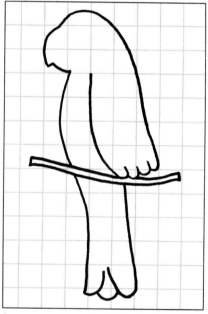

1 square equals 1 1/16 inch

Skier from a Pod

Follow the scrap-crafter's credo: If you can't find the thing you want, want the thing you find. The hardy sweet gum of the genus Liquidambar grows across most of the United States, and its globular pod is therefore widely available. Any pod similarly shaped could be substituted, even a pinecone might work.

Materials:

1 liquidambar (sweet gum) pod
   for body
1 whole walnut for head
White tacky glue
Felt scraps
2 sequins
2 wooden toothpicks
2 black half beads for eyes
Fabric scraps
Dark-color art paper for skis
6″ gold cord for hanger (optional)

Instructions:

To make skier's body, remove a few spines from one end of the pod, to provide a slightly scooped out area to hold walnut. Glue nut and pod together. Let dry. *To make a scarf,* cut a ⅜ inch x 6 inch strip of felt and taper strip at each end to a point. Glue scarf in place around neckline, where walnut and pod are joined. *To make ski poles,* glue sequins to pointed ends of toothpicks as shown in photo. Glue toothpicks to sides of pod. *For mittens,* cut two small triangles from felt and glue over middle of ski poles on sides of pod. Glue eyes in place in middle of walnut. Cut *hat* from fabric scraps, using pattern as guide. Glue side A to side B, right sides together. Let dry. Turn right-side-out, fold under raw edge, and place on top of walnut. Glue in place to hold. *To make skis,* cut two strips of art paper, ⅜ inch x 2½ inches. Glue strips together in middle, overlapping to form an X.

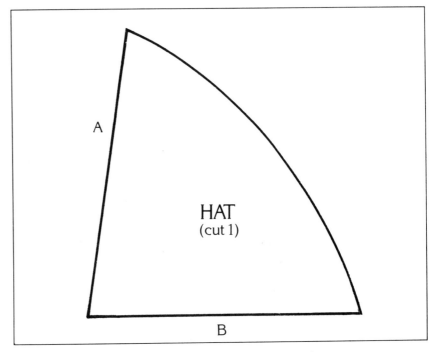

A

HAT
(cut 1)

B

Glue to bottom of pod. Curl tips of skis around a pencil to give them shape. Tie gold cord to hat, if desired. Use as Christmas tree ornament, package topper, party favor at a ski-crowd reunion, etc.

Pod Wreath

Materials:

7 liquidambar (sweet gum) pods
1 yd. 1″-wide ribbon
Hot glue
6″ gold cord for hanger

Instructions:

Remove a few spines from both sides of each pod with kitchen shears. This will give you a flat area where pods can be attached. Glue pods together with hot glue in a circle to form wreath. Wrap ribbon around wreath as shown in photo, covering each joint. Tie ribbon in a bow at top. Tie hanger to top of wreath.

Snowman for all Seasons

Materials:

2 liquidambar (sweet gum) pods for body
Hot glue
2 moving eyes, 7mm.
1 red plastic berry for nose
2 beads ¼″ diameter for buttons
White tacky glue
Scrap white paper for mouth
Scrap black construction paper for hat
6″ gold cord for hanger

Instructions:

For body, glue two pods together with hot glue. It's easier to attach them if you remove a few spines at the joining point. Using photo as guide, glue eyes, nose, and buttons in place with tacky glue. Cut *mouth* shape from plain white paper, following pattern. Glue in place. *For hat,* cut circle 1¼ inches diameter and a strip ¾ inch x 2 inches from black construction paper. Overlap strip ¼ inch. Glue together forming tube shape. Glue tube in middle of circle forming hat. Glue hat in place on top of head, again removing a few prickles at joining point. *For scarf,* cut strip of fabric scrap ⅜ inch x 3 inches, following pattern. Wrap scarf around snowman's neck, overlapping at side of neck, and glue in place.

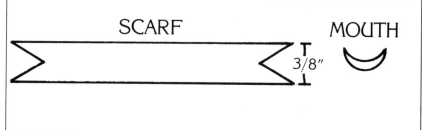

SCARF   MOUTH   3/8″

Pig from a Pod

Materials:

5 wooden toothpicks
1 liquidambar (sweet gum) pod
   for body
Small piece black felt for nose
   and ears
2 white plastic eyes
Black acrylic paint
1½"-piece 26-gauge covered wire
   for tail
6" gold cord for hanger (optional)

Instructions:

For pig's legs, cut off point at one end of each toothpick. Paint each toothpick black. Let dry. Glue toothpicks into a hole in pod as shown in photo, making sure

EAR
(cut 2)

pod body will stand straight on toothpicks. Let glue dry. *For nose,* cut ½ inch x 1 inch black felt. Roll and glue to hold. Glue nose into place, using picture as guide. Remove a few prickles from pod around eye area to flatten it enough to hold eyes. Glue *eyes* into place close together. Let dry. Place a small eye of black paint in

center of white dot. *For ears,* cut black felt, following pattern. Glue in place using photo as guide. *For tail,* cut 1-inch piece of wire. Paint wire black. Let dry. Coil wire around a toothpick to shape into corkscrew. Remove toothpick and glue tail in place on back of pod. Glue hanger to top of pod, if desired.

Cone Flower Girl

Materials:

⅙ yd. 3"-wide burlap ribbon for
   skirt
1½" pinecone for body
Fabric scraps for scarf and apron
White tacky glue
1" piece white chenille stem
1 hazelnut about ¾" diameter for
   head
⅙ yd. yarn or ribbon for necktie
Dried flower spray
6" gold cord for hanger

Instructions:

Using pattern as guide, cut

skirt from burlap ribbon and glue around middle of pinecone. Cut *apron and scarf* from fabric scraps, using pattern as guide. Glue apron to front of skirt at waistline. *To make hands,* fold chenille stem in half. Center above apron and glue between layers of pinecone. *For head,* glue hazelnut to top of pinecone. Let dry. Glue *scarf* in place on top of head. Tie yarn or ribbon around neck for trim. Slip stems of flowers between hands and glue in place. Glue gold cord to back of head for hanger.

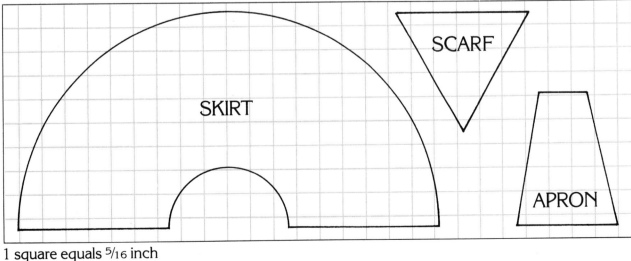

SCARF

SKIRT

APRON

1 square equals ⁵⁄₁₆ inch

Cornhusk Tree

CORNHUSK CREATIVITY

Use clean green husks trimmed from fresh ears of corn and prepare them in one of the following ways:

1. Soak the husks in a basin containing 2 quarts water and 2 teaspoons glycerin. When husks have absorbed the glycerin, let dry flat on sheets of newspaper. The glycerin keeps the husks permanently supple.

2. To change the color of the husks, dye them with fabric dye in the color of your choice, following package directions, and let dry before use. Or bleach them in the sun to a lovely pale tint, turning them for even bleaching.

Long-lasting and dramatic, this is the special something to give to the family that has everything. You can often find plywood scraps at the lumberyard: Get one as close to the size indicated as possible but don't worry about several inches one way or another, provided the overall proportion is pleasing.

Materials:

⅛″ thick plywood about 22″ x 32″, or corrugated cardboard pieces
Electric saw, drill (optional)
Heavy-duty stapler or staple gun
White tacky glue
Wire hanger
Wire cutters
Sharp knife or single-edged razor blade
Approx. 100 glycerinized cornhusks (see box)
Approx. 30 miniature pinecones (see page 8 for how to prepare sticky cones)
About 20 stalks dried wheat
1″ x 2″ x 2″ block plastic foam
26-gauge bare wire
Florist's moss or brown paint to conceal foam

Instructions:

Have the tree shape cut at the lumberyard when you buy plywood, or cut at home with an electric saw. If you use pieces of corrugated cardboard from cartons, staple or glue them together in tree shape. The tree shown is 22 inches at its widest point, tapering to 32 inches high including a 7 inch x 7 inch base. Attach wire hanger with stapler, or drill a hole through wood or cardboard, then wire it on.

Cut the husks into 1½-inch-wide strips, and fold each strip into a loop 2½ inches high. Starting at the top, staple one loop to the tree frame, then continue stapling the edge of each loop, following the photo. Overlap the

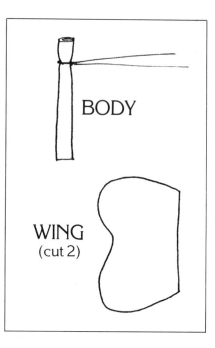

BODY

WING (cut 2)

loops to cover the preceding staples in each row as you work. Continue this procedure down both sides of the tree to cover the entire tree and base. Note placement of loops on base: they are upside-down; start stapling from the bottom up. Reserve five or six of the largest pinecones. Trim tree with remaining pinecones, gluing them on. Make a cluster of the reserved pinecones (see instructions page 158). Force stem of cluster into frame.

For the wheat spray, attach block of plastic foam to the base with wire. Conceal foam by covering it with moss or painting it brown. Place wheat into foam as shown in design. To force stems into foam, you will need to make a hole in the foam first, or you can wire a small wooden toothpick to each stem to reinforce before forcing into foam. You can dip the wood picks and stem of cluster into the tacky glue before forcing them into the foam, to be sure they stay firmly in place.

Make *birds or butterflies* for the center of the wheat spray. To make the butterflies shown, use a piece of cornhusk 3 inches x 4 inches for each butterfly (you need two). Roll into a tube for the *body*. For the head, wrap a wire ½ inch from one end (see drawing). To shape the head, use your scissors to slightly round the end. Cut the *wings* from a flat husk, following pattern. (Pick a husk with texture for best results.) Using tacky glue, secure wings to body. Let dry. Glue or wire the two butterflies onto the arrangement.

DESIGNING WITH DRIED FLOWERS AND LEAVES

Dried flowers, foliages, weeds, and grasses are an extraordinarily versatile craft material. You can paste them on greeting cards, invitations, or stationery; arrange them in vases for home decoration; cluster and use them as package trims; press them under glass to make flower pictures; or insert them into plastic foam balls or eggs as Christmas or Easter ornaments. And flowers and leaves are yours as a gift from nature, a material available the year around if you preserve them by any of the following methods.

Preserving Plant Materials

Always pick and dry twice as many flowers and leaves as you need to allow for loss in the drying process. Select varied shapes, sizes, and even stages of growth, from bud to open blooms, to give you the greatest flexibility when you design.

The preservation process depends on removing all moisture from the plant material, and the faster the moisture is removed, the more color it retains. Most blooms will dry within two weeks, but this varies with the original moisture content, the bulk of the blossom, etc. Since the timing is inexact, you will have to keep checking on a trial-and-error basis. The most popular methods of preservation follow.

Pressing. Lay plant material flat and separated on several sheets of newspaper or paper toweling in phone book. Cover with more sheets. Each layer of material should be separated with newspaper sheets. Press with weights (bricks, heavy cans, etc.). Turn weekly until dry, changing newspaper sheets if necessary.

Hanging. Tie fresh flowers (leaves removed) loosely at their stems with string. Hang heads down by bunches of a half dozen or so from hooks or wire hangers (making certain they do not touch), in a dry, dark closet or attic. Many flowers and herbs respond well to this method.

Air-drying. Plants like hydrangea with dense flower clusters dry naturally in a flower arrangement, when the less-enduring types have been discarded. Just let them stand upright in the container, out of sunlight. Add no more water, and they should be dry within two weeks.

In a drying mixture. Pour about 2 inches of one of the following mixtures into a shallow airtight container. Insert flowers (leaves removed) and foliages so they do not touch. Sprinkle more mixture on top until flowers are covered but not buried. Leave stems exposed and upright, except in silica gel mixture. Sculptured flowers (daffodil, foxglove, gloxinia, etc.) will hold their shape if you gently sift more mixture into their petals, smoothing out any which become twisted. Check each week or so until flowers are dry. Gently pour off mixture, saving it to be reused if you wish, and gently clean flowers with soft brush.

Borax and cornmeal mixture. Combine one-third borax with two-thirds cornmeal. A large box of borax and three or four large boxes of cornmeal will be enough for a start.

Borax and sand mixture. Use half fine sand and half borax.

Silica gel. Absorbs moisture quickest, so flowers retain most color, but is the most expensive material. Container holding flowers during the drying process must be nonporous, tightly covered, and sealed with freezer tape, or this thirsty chemical will pick up moisture from the air. Test after three days to see if flowers have dried.

Glycerinizing. Use a tall jar. Fill it with a solution of one part glycerin to two parts water to a depth of 6 inches. Place foliage stems, freshly cut, in jar. Do not cover. Let stand in airy place for about two weeks. Leaves will absorb the solution if they are gathered at their peak, and become pliable and long-lasting with an interesting depth of color. Try barberry, beech, crabapple, dock, eucalyptus, jacaranda, magnolia, oak, and even lunaria and Chinese lanterns.

Flowers and Foliage to Dry, by Color

The number of flowers that can be preserved is almost limitless, so experiment with the blossoms, weeds, leaves, shrubs, vines, pods, etc., available to you. Here's a list to get you started. The preservation process is specified in parentheses.

White: Baby's breath (H). Dahlia (M). Daisy (M). Honesty (H, G). Magnolia (M). Queen Anne's lace (M). Spirea (M). Statice (H). Yarrow (H; foliage P).

Tan: Columbine (M). Daffodil (M). Ferns, picked after frost (P). Palm leaves (P, A). Sea oats (P). Wheat (H, A).

Pink: Astilbe (P, H, M). Baby's breath (H). Carnation (M). Cosmos (P, M). Crepe myrtle (H, M). Larkspur (M). Painted daisy (P, M). Peony (M). Torch ginger (H).

Lavender, Purple: Amaranthus (H). Foxglove (M). Hollyhock (H, A). Pansy (P). Ranuncula (M). Stock (M). Violet (P, M).

Yellow, Gold: Acacia (P, H). Pods (M). Celosia (H). Chrysanthemum (H, M). Goldenrod (H). Marigold (M). Rose (M). Tansy (H). Yarrow (H).

Green: Bells of Ireland (A). Ferns, picked in June (P). Hydrangea (H, A). Scotch broom (H). Many other leaves (P, M).

Blue: Aster (P, M). Ageratum (M). Delphinium (M). Globe thistle (H). Larkspur (M). Lilac (M). Scilla (P). Salvia (P, H).

Orange: Calendula (M). Globe amaranth (H). Marigold (H, M). Strawflower (H, A). Zinnia (M).

Red: Bittersweet berries (H). Celosia (H). Chinese lantern pod (H)—cut along veins into sections for lovely translucent material. Coleus (P). Maple leaf (P, M). Sumac foliage (P, H).

G = Glycerinizing
P = Pressing
H = Hanging
A = Air-drying
M = Immerse in drying mixture

Storing Dried Materials

Flat cardboard boxes are easily stored. Place heavy blossoms on bottom. Separate delicate dried flowers with layers of waxed paper. Seal with tape to make airtight. Small dried materials can be sealed in plastic containers with air-tight lids. Store in dry place. Label and date the contents so you'll remember what you have.

Hint for Using Dried Materials

If dried material has lost its stem, make an artificial stem using a piece of 26-gauge wire. Hook the wire into the blossom or twist it through the calyx. Or lay a piece of toothpick or wire alongside the stub of the stem and tape them together with florist's tape. There are no hard-and-fast rules: Anything goes as long as it works.

Petal Painting

Almost everyone during a lifetime has placed a treasured flower, corsage, or leaf specimen between the pages of a book to "save" it, and garden clubbers are familiar with the craft of drying and pressing flowers in arrangements. Now, a unique idea is shared with us by June Peterson, a talented designer, who takes the flowers apart, petal by petal, and reassembles them in subtle flower paintings or collages... delicate flower arrangements with an airy translucence unlike any you have ever seen. Even the vase is made by overlapping paper-thin petals.

What flowers are used in these lovely designs? Any that dry well. A favorite with June Peterson is the ranunculus (buttercup). Its colors stay vivid, and one flower head yields many petals that dry sturdy though almost transparent. June also recommends ranunculus petals for fashioning vases, as shown in our photo. She often mixes flower types in the same design (for example, a wisteria blossom hanging from a honeysuckle vine); even if this is horticulturally inexact, it is aesthetically most pleasing.

Materials:

Assorted dried flowers and petals, leaves, stems, and branches
Mat board for matting and background. (Choose any color mat board that harmonizes with the petals; soft pastels are pleasing.)
Single-edged razor blade
Tweezers
Pencil and paper
Soft cloth
Frame (optional)

Instructions:

Lay out the design of the flowers and vase in light pencil outline on the mat or a separate sheet of paper, or work without a fixed pattern (see design suggestions below). Then test your design with the flower petals themselves. Since each leaf, petal, and stem is solidly glued to the mat board and cannot be lifted, you must know exactly where it is to go and what it will look like before you fix it in place. For best results, test and trace each assemblage of flowers on a separate sheet before you attempt to recompose it and glue it in place.

But before you build up the flowers, you must create the vase. Test first. Then spread tacky glue all over the vase traced on the mat. Lay down the petals, overlapping as shown in the photo. *Cut away any excess petals from the outline with single-edged razor blade.* Use a soft cloth to mop up any excess glue that seeps out from under the materials. You might find a pair of tweezers a handy tool to use in lifting and placing petals. When the vase is done, glue in the branches of leaves at the outer edges of the design. Then gradually fill in the painting with petals, finishing with the four large focal flowers.

Let dry thoroughly and then frame, if desired. Do not hang picture in direct sunlight.

Design Suggestions for Flower Paintings:

1. Place the plant material in vase so that it seems to be growing from one common source or branch. Take a tip from nature: some stems should curve right, others left; some be seen full view, others to the side; no two blossoms exactly at the same height.

2. Establish the overall silhouette with the long lines of foliage; the lighter weight or smaller leaves and flowers on the longest stems should be set in first, at the outermost areas of the design: top, sides, or trailing from the vase (like the branch at the lower left in our photo). Then fill in the flowers leading to the center of interest.

3. Finish with the largest, most brilliant, most important blossoms or group of blossoms at the center of interest, generally the place in the design where the stems of the plant material appear to be entering the opening of the vase.

4. In general, the vase should occupy about one-third of the total arrangement, the plant material two-thirds.

5. Do experiment! You'll soon learn which petals give your paintings just the texture you want. For the wood-grain look of a basket, try cutting petals from white or yellow roses into strips, using a razor blade to give the effect of weaving. Petals dried to a tan-brown will give a wood effect if overlapped to follow a typical wood grain. Unlike painting, you don't have to worry about shading, as the petals and plant materials create their own natural contrasts in tone and texture.

Preserved-Flower Hanging Heart

Hang your heart-shaped bouquet where your heart is! Here's a lovely keepsake to make for your spouse as an anniversary gift, for Valentine's Day, or for any other sentimental occasion. The basic procedure we give here—*learning to use florist's tape correctly*—is also the key to making corsages, bouquets, garlands, and wreaths that have a professional finish.

Materials:

12″ length bare or covered 18-gauge wire
Roll of green ½″ florist's tape
Dried statice, baby's breath, or other small sprays
Dried or artificial berries
Five 1-yard lengths ⅜″-wide ribbon

Instructions:

Bend the wire into the shape of a heart. Now hold the wire frame, with the spool of tape on top of it, between thumb and forefinger of left hand. Hold the loose end of the tape with the right hand. Wrap tape twice around the point where wire ends join. Twirl the wire, stretching the tape and guiding it on a slight diagonal as you twirl, to wrap. Use as little tape as possible; try to avoid too much overlapping of the tape but be sure to cover all the wire. If your first efforts are not as smooth as you would like, press the tape into place to get rid of the bumps. Select a dried berry or flower spray, lay it against the wire, and tape the stems to the wire, stretching the tape and guiding it along the wire as you twirl it. With the roll of tape still attached to the wire, add a second flower or berry spray to conceal the first stem, and at a slightly different angle to give volume to the design. Continue until the entire heart is covered as shown in photo, then wrap the tape twice around the finish point and cut or pull off the roll of tape.

Tie one length of ribbon to the top of design for a hanger. To make streamers on bottom, place remaining four lengths of ribbon one on top of the other and fold at center. Place center on bottom of heart, and bring ends together down under the frame, around the back and up, through the design and over the wire, ending by pulling under the center of ribbon through the fold; this ties the streamers in place (see photo).

Homemade Paper and Botanical Print

Materials (makes three 8″ x 11″ sheets of paper):

1 quart materials to "recycle":
leaves, flowers, straw, pine
needles, white paper towels,
scrap paper (paper is necessary
for pulp to form; use 3
shredded paper towels per
quart)
1 envelope plain unflavored
gelatin powder
Large dishpan
Screen approx. 9″ x 12″ (old
window screening stapled to
frame of scrap wood)
Sponge
Newspaper sheets
Iron
Dried flowers, leaves, ferns for
print
Acrylic paint
Frame (optional)

Instructions:

To make paper, tear material to recycle into small pieces and shred in blender or mixer in batches. Add a cup or so of water, along with gelatin powder. Blend until pulp forms. This mixture is called slurry. Pour slurry into dishpan containing 3 to 4 inches of water. Dip screen into dishpan by holding screen perpendicular to pan, screen side toward you. Slide screen under slurry and bring it up toward you horizontally so that water can drain, leaving mash on top of screen (frame side will be facing down). Sponge off excess slurry on all edges of screen to create a deckle edge. The wet mixture adheres to the screen because of the water; remove excess water by sponging underside of screen. Flip screen over onto flat surface covered with newspapers (frame side is now facing up). Continue to sponge up excess water through screen. Carefully remove paper by raising and gently tapping screen. If paper will not come off, sponge again and let paper fall from screen onto newspaper-covered surface. (Do not attempt to lift paper until dry—it could easily tear.) Cover paper with second sheet of newsprint or paper towel. Press the paper with an iron until it dries, or squeeze moisture out by pressing with heavy books. Let dry completely (approximately twenty-four hours). When dry, peel back the newsprint to remove the homemade paper.

To make a botanical print, arrange flowers, leaves, and ferns into a pleasing design. Brush acrylic paint onto flowers, leaves, and ferns and place them facedown on your homemade paper. Cover plants with paper towel and press hard with a heavy book; lift off plants and paint imprint will remain.

Homemade paper can also be used to make cards, stationery, bookmarks, and the like.

Victorian Seed House

Whether you are creating something simple or elaborate, gathering and preserving the natural materials for seed pictures is half the fun. (If gathering is impossible for you, your supermarket can supply most of the ingredients called for.) If pine needles are not available, substitute trimmed pieces of cattail or other stems or twigs. In the seed house shown, the pine needles used vertically are about 1½ inches long; the horizontal ones are about 4 inches long.

Materials:

11″ x 14″ cardboard (shirt size) for backing
Small cardboard for "squeegy"
Toothpick
Tweezers
Frame
Natural materials:
Dried pine needles for fence and house siding
Caraway seeds for roof, approximately 1 teaspoon
Fennel seeds for roof, approximately 1 teaspoon
Straw for porch trim, stairs, front doors
Salt for clouds, approximately 1 tablespoon
Salt dyed with blue food color for sky, approximately 4 tablespoons
Dried, crushed thyme for grass, approximately 2 tablespoons
Celery salt for walkway, approximately 1 tablespoon
Assorted flower seeds for trim
Dried baby's breath or similar material for trees
Dried, crushed basil leaves for bushes, approximately 1 whole teaspoon

Instructions:

Using photograph as a guide, draw pattern onto cardboard backing. Work a small section at a time, first applying glue, then natural materials. Use tweezers and a toothpick to help pick up and place seeds. Start with the house. Apply glue to frame the windows, press the pine needles in place. Following photo, continue to fill in roof and house area, using straw and caraway and fennel seeds.

Next, use a second small piece of cardboard as a "squeegy" to apply an even coat of glue over the sky and grass areas. Apply dyed salt for sky and plain salt for clouds. Using crushed thyme, fill in glued grass area. Use celery salt for glued walkway border. Continuing to follow photo, glue two pine needles horizontally on each side of walkway to form base of fence. Glue next pieces vertically across over base pieces to give depth to fence. Finish project by gluing basil and dried baby's breath, following photo, for trees and bushes on each side of stairs. Let dry overnight and frame.

CHAPTER TWO

Pretty Paper Projects

Anyone with average dexterity and patience can make designs from paper to be proudly displayed in the home year-round or during the holiday season. Your source of materials is unlimited, from plain typewriter paper to old letters, doilies, newspapers, magazines, and paper plates, and you have a wide variety of shapes and colors to draw from.

With paper so plentiful and the price so right, we could fill our "scrap-craft" book with this material alone. But we've been selective and as varied as possible to give you some inkling of the wide range of designs that are possible: wreaths, nosegays, and decorations for the holidays, plant containers, flowers, quite a few darling animal figures and other paper sculptures, tissue-paper paintings and collages, and, finally, some jewelry made of newspaper that we're especially proud of. So start collecting.

Angels from Doilies

These adorable angels, quick and easy to assemble and very inexpensive, can be used as Christmas tree ornaments, table decorations, mobile pendants, or package-toppers. Without wings, they could be used as figures and dolls for many different special occasions such as brides on top of wedding gifts, or a group of figures dancing around a maypole.

Materials:

24" yellow 2-ply yarn, threaded on needle, for hair
1 wooden bead ⅝" diameter for head
Permanent fine-line black marking pen
3" piece of 22-gauge wire or chenille stem
White tacky glue
1 round white 4" paper doily for skirt
1 round white 2½" paper doily for wings
Gold cord for hanger (optional)

Instructions:

To make angel's hair, thread yarn on needle through bead, leaving approximately 1 inch at end to hold on to. Bring needle around and through bead in same direction, repeat approximately nine times until yarn covers about two-thirds of the bead. Cut yarn attached to needle approximately 2 inches from bead. *For bun* on top of angel's head, apply a small dab of glue around base of 2-inch piece of yarn. Starting from the center, coil yarn around in a circle forming bun. Tuck end under bun, securing with a dab of glue. Place wire or chenille stem into bead head for neck. Draw *eyes, nose, and mouth* on bead with the black marking pen, as shown in the drawing. *For the skirt,* cut the 4-inch doily in half. Glue one half into a cone shape.

To make the wings, cut two quarter sections from the 2½-inch doily. Glue wings to cone ½ inch from top. Insert wire neck down through the center of the cone body and glue or staple to hold head in place. Let dry. Glue hanger to hair, if desired.

Nosegay Doily Wreath

(See next page for instructions.)

This wreath is fragile in appearance but very sturdy, and feminine to the last paper doily and tiny nosegay.

23

Materials:

12″ beveled plastic foam wreath
5 yds. 1½″-wide red ribbon to
    cover wreath
White tacky glue
Sixteen 4″ paper doilies
3 yds. ¼″ red ribbon for bows
24 ribbon floribunda roses (see
    instructions page 160)
24 miniature pinecone clusters
    with artificial berries (from
    craft shop, or see instructions
    page 158)
Dried baby's-breath
1 roll white ½″ florist's tape
1 chenille stem for hanger

Instructions:

Wrap plastic foam wreath with 1½″-wide ribbon. Secure end of ribbon to wreath with glue. Cut eight of the doilies in half. Fan-fold at ½-inch intervals, as shown in drawing. Rejoining the two half pieces, space the doilies evenly around wreath (see photo), gluing in place. Tie small bows from the ¼-inch ribbon and glue the bows onto the wreath where the two halves of doilies meet, as shown in drawing. Cut 1-inch wedge from each of the remaining doilies. Overlap cut edges ¼ inch and glue to form slight cone shape.

To assemble nosegays, hold three ribbon roses, add three pinecone clusters between roses, evenly spaced, and three sprigs of baby's breath, evenly spaced, using photograph as guide. Tape ends together smoothly with florist's tape, to make one stem. Cut taped stem to 1 inch. Slip stem through center of doily cone. (Tip of cone might have to be snipped off to allow stem to fit through.) Assemble eight nosegays in this manner. Space nosegays evenly

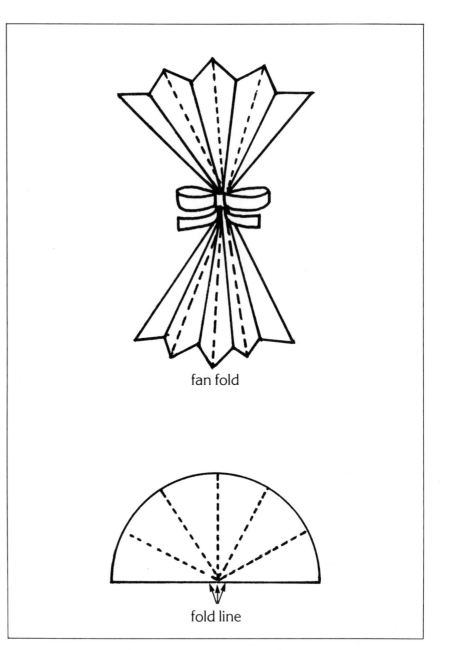

fan fold

fold line

around wreath between doily fans and insert stems into wreath. Dip ends of stems into glue before inserting into wreath, for best hold. (Note: If it is difficult to push stems through ribbon covering wreath, use sharp tool such as end of scissors to punch a hole through ribbon, then insert glued stems into wreath.) Attach hanger made of chenille stem to back of wreath.

Doily nosegays can also be used individually as decorations or attached to plastic foam forms to make centerpieces or displays.

24

Muffin Cup Wreath

If you thought muffin cup liners had limited uses, here's a yummy design to prove otherwise.

Materials:

About 250 assorted-color paper muffin cups 2½" diameter
12½" beveled plastic foam wreath
1 package 26-gauge wire
White tacky glue
Spray glue
Fine diamond-dust glitter
Optional trimmings: Christmas balls, satin ribbons.
Chenille stem for hanger

Instructions:

Fold muffin cups in half and then fan-fold as shown for Nosegay Doily Wreath (page 24) for fluffiness. Grasp bottom point of folded cup and wrap with wire. Snip wire to 1 inch. Dip end of wire in glue and press into wreath. Starting with outside row and working toward inside of wreath, row by row, continue to attach folded and wired cups to wreath. When wreath is completely covered with muffin cups, spray entire wreath with spray glue and sprinkle with diamond-dust glitter. Give a top coat of spray glue as a final coat to hold glitter. Let dry. *To trim wreath,* if desired wire three Christmas balls together with wire and attach to wreath; see photograph as guide for placement. Tie ribbon bows, attach wire to backs of bows, and attach to wreath, again using photograph as guide for placement. Glue hanger made of chenille stem to back of wreath.

Paper Plate Flowers

Materials:

1 white 12″ paper plate with
    fluted edges for flowers
Small sheets of colored art paper:
    dark green and light green for
    leaves, yellow for flower
    centers, blue for background
White tacky glue
Scissors
Pinking shears (optional)
Stylus or dry pen point
Pencil
Compass to mark circles
Frame (optional)

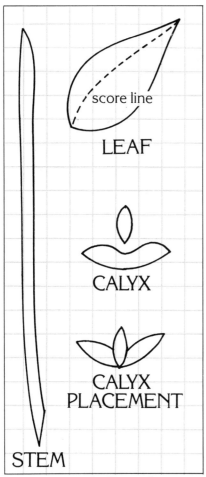

1 square equals ⁶/₁₆ inch

Instructions:

Cut petals 1¼ inches long from
entire edge of paper plate. Taper
to a point at flat end. Cut two
leaves and one stem from dark

green art paper and three leaves,
one stem, and calyx from light
green art paper, using patterns as
guide. Clip edges of leaves with
pinking shears or regular shears
to give texture. Score center line
of leaves with stylus or dry pen
point. Slightly fold along score
line to give shape. Lightly mark
blue background paper for flower
and leaf placement, using photo
as guide. *To make large flowers,*
starting with bottom layer of petals, glue in circle, using a circle ½
inch in diameter as gluing guide
line. Continue to glue two more
layers of petals in circle, working
toward center, alternating placement of each layer to give depth
to flower. Glue three petals, ½
inch in length, evenly spaced in
center for final layer. Glue five
yellow art paper circles ¼ inch in
diameter in a circle and one in
middle, for center of flower (see
photo). *To make bud,* glue three
petals, 1¼ inches in length, in
place as shown in photo, overlapping at bottom, fanning out at
top. Glue four petals over first
layer, alternating placement, finishing with one petal for final
layer, directly in middle. Glue the
two calyx pieces together, as
shown in drawing. Slightly curl
calyx and glue on side at bottom
of bud. Glue stems in place using
photo as guide. Note that stems
are glued only at top and bottom
and are arched to give depth.
Glue leaves in place. Frame, if desired.

Paper Plate Lamb

Materials:

Yellow construction paper for
　background
1 white 12″ paper plate with
　fluted edges
Paper hole puncher (optional)
Pink construction paper for
　cheeks
White tacky glue
Permanent fine-line black
　marking pen
Frame (optional)

Instructions:

Trace pattern full size onto yellow construction paper. Cut petals from edge of paper plate as follows: thirty-five petals ¾ inch long; six petals 1¼ inches long, tapered to a point at flat end (two for ears, four for legs); three petals ½ inch long, tapered to a point at flat end (between ears); one petal ¾ inch long, tapered at both ends for tail.

Cut two circles ¼ inch in diameter from pink construction paper for cheeks (we've used a hole puncher). Using pattern as a guide, draw feet on four 1¼-inch petals for legs with marking pen. Glue legs in place on yellow background paper. Next, glue five petals ¾ inch long in a row vertically above front legs. Continue working toward tail, gluing five more rows, gluing the tip of each petal under the row in front of it. Glue tail in place. Cut face from center of paper plate, using pattern as guide. Draw eyes, nose, and mouth on face with marking pen. Glue pink paper cheeks in place. Glue face in place. Glue two petals 1¼ inches long in place for ears. Glue three petals ½ inch long between ears as shown in pattern. Frame, if desired.

1 square equals ⁵/₁₆ inch

Antiqued Plant Containers from Paper

If you're worried about eventual water seepage, put plant in a plastic container before inserting it in this handmade decorative one.

Container #1

Materials:

Newspaper
White tacky glue
Cardboard plant or paint bucket
Stiff brush for glue
Acrylic paint: light brown and dark brown (several bright colors for trim, optional)
Spray or brush-on glaze

Instructions:

Cut strips of newspaper 2 inches wide, the length of the newspaper. Fold strips in half lengthwise. Glue vertical strips of newspaper to top of bucket, extending approximately 1½ inches to inside of bucket over rim. Space strips approximately ¼ inch apart, leaving ends hanging down the side. *To weave horizontal strips,* start at top edge of bucket and weave strips in and out of vertical strips, gluing in place as you go. Note that strips do not have to lie completely flat against the bucket; wrinkles add depth and texture to project. Continue to weave horizontal strips until entire surface is covered. Turn ends of vertical strips under bottom of bucket and glue down. Using a stiff brush, apply coat of glue over entire surface of woven newspaper, following weave pattern, leaving horizontal brush strokes in horizontal strips and vertical brush strokes in vertical strips. Let dry. Paint with light brown acrylic paint. Let dry. Paint design around top in bright colors, if desired. Let dry. Antique, following instructions for Container #3.

Container #2

Materials:

Newspaper
White tacky glue
Cardboard plant or paint bucket
Lace trim
Acrylic paint: light brown, dark brown, and several bright colors of your choice for trim
Spray or brush-on glaze

Instructions:

Cut newspaper into strips approximately 1¼ inches wide, tear into 2-inch lengths. Fold first row of strips in half lengthwise and glue over lip of bucket. Glue next row of strips on bucket, overlapping first row ¼ inch. Continue overlapping rows, covering entire bucket surface and bottom lip of bucket. Glue lace trim around upper edge. Let dry. Paint entire surface with light brown acrylic paint. Let dry. Add detail to lace trim by dipping end of toothpick into several bright colors of acrylic paint and dotting on to make flowers. Let dry. Antique surface, following instructions for Container #3.

Container #3

Materials:

4 sheets textured paper toweling, each 9" x 11"
White tacky glue
Cardboard plant or paint bucket
Lace trim
Acrylic paint: light brown, dark brown, and white
Spray or brush-on glaze

Instructions:

Cut paper towels lengthwise in strips, varied from 1 inch to 1¼ inches wide each. Apply a coat of glue to entire outside surface of bucket. Glue strips of paper towels vertically around bucket, extending over top and bottom lip. Apply coat of glue over paper towels. Glue lace around upper and lower edges. Let dry. Paint entire surface of bucket light brown. Let dry. Paint lace white. Let dry. *To antique container,* test dark brown paint on small inside surface. If paints are compatible (second paint should lie smoothly on base coat, with no buckling or lifting), apply the dark brown paint on outside surface, a small section at a time, *immediately* wiping off with soft cloth so dark brown color remains only in cracks and crevices. Let dry. Seal surface with coat of glaze and allow to dry in dust-free area.

Butterfly Planter Sticks

Pretty plant sticks with space down the body for labeling if you wish, made from cut-out paper. Nice for mobiles, too.

Materials:

Colored art paper (one 8″ square sheet for each butterfly)
18-gauge white-covered wire (one 18″-length for each butterfly)
X-acto knife
Acrylic paint (coordinating with or matching paper colors)
White tacky glue

Instructions:

Fold art paper in half and lightly trace the pattern, following suggested cutouts or designing your own. Cut out with X-acto knife. Unfold and flatten. Paint covered wire with paint. Let dry. Glue wire in place the length of butterfly's body. Let dry. Bend wire just below butterfly's tail as shown in photo. Bend wings upward to give shape to butterfly.

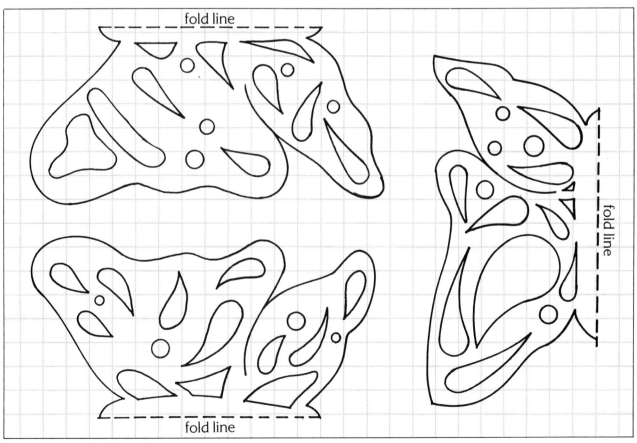

1 square equals ⁵/₁₆ inch

Art Paper Mouse

Materials:

X-acto knife, single-edged razor
    blade, or scissors
Colored art paper (2 coordinating
    or contrasting colors for each
    mouse)
White tacky glue

Instructions:

Lightly trace the pattern, body
on one color of art paper and ears,
eyes, nose, and tail pieces on another color. Cut out. Insert tail B
into slot B on body. Insert ears A
into slots A on body. Glue edge C
to D forming body (cone shape).
Cut and glue eyes in place using
photo as guide for size and placement.

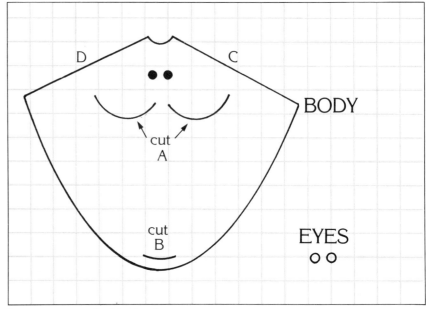

1 square equals ⁵/₁₆ inch

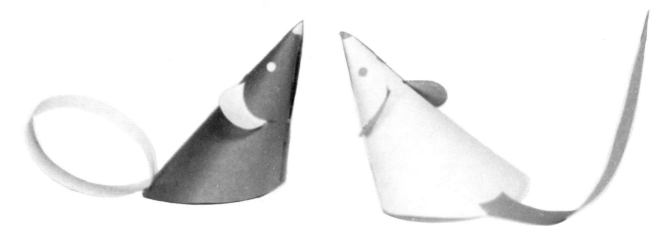

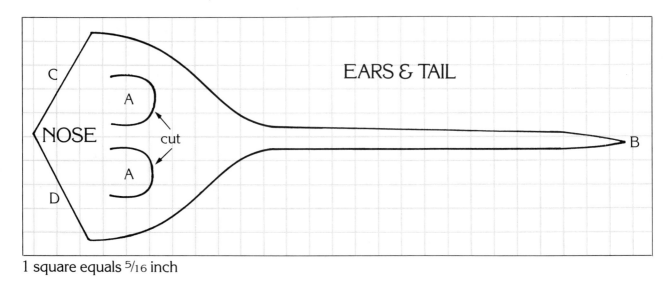

1 square equals ⁵/₁₆ inch

Art Paper Elephant

How would you like a parade of these sculptured animals on a birthday-party table?

Materials:

Art paper: blue for body, head, and eye centers; green for ears and eye backs
1 plastic flexible straw
White tacky glue
Stylus or dry pen point
Paper hole puncher or X-acto knife

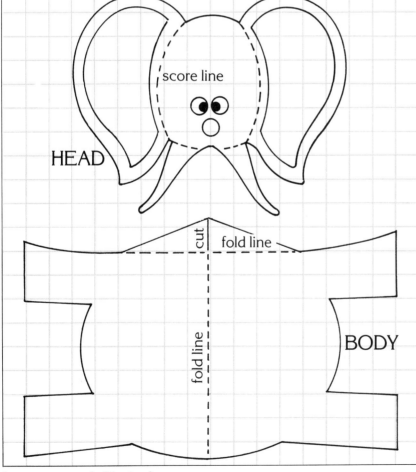

score line

HEAD

cut

fold line

fold line

fold line

BODY

1 square equals 7/16 inch

Instructions:

Lightly trace pattern onto art paper: body, head, and eye centers on blue art paper; ears and eye back from green art paper. Cut them out. Grasp both ends of straw and pull pleats out to extend straw. Measure and cut off at an angle 1¼ inch of straw at end closest to flex. Cut 2 inches off other end of straw, at a reverse angle to nose cut, to form body and tail section. Fold body down middle, where indicated on pattern. Glue body in place over long end of straw. Let dry. While body is drying, glue ears and eyes in place on head. Using dotted line as guide, score elephant's head with a stylus or pen point. Slightly bend ears forward. Using a hole puncher or X-acto knife, cut out trunk hole. Insert straw through back of head and glue back of head to body at folded edges. Bend straw down at flex to give shape to trunk.

Art Paper Giraffe

Materials:

1 plastic flexible straw for neck and body
Art paper: white for body; hot pink for spots, toenails, ears, horn, nose, eye center; yellow for eye backs
White tacky glue
Paper hole puncher

Instructions:

Grasp both ends of straw and pull pleats out to extend. Measure and cut 6¾ inches from end closest to flex. Lightly trace pattern onto art paper: body on white art paper; spots, toenails, horns, nose, and eye centers on hot pink paper; eye backs on yellow paper. Cut out. (Hint: We used a hole puncher for nose, horns, and eye backs.) Glue spots and toenails to white body. Let dry. Fold body down middle as indicated on pattern. Glue ears, eyes, and horns to head, using pattern as guide. Let dry. Glue side A to side B forming cone-shaped head. Let dry. Using a hole puncher, punch hole in back of head at neckline

to insert top of straw into head. Glue nose in place. Bend straw to a 90-degree angle. Glue body in place over the short end of straw and insert straw into head at other end, using photo as a guide. Adjust flex for balance.

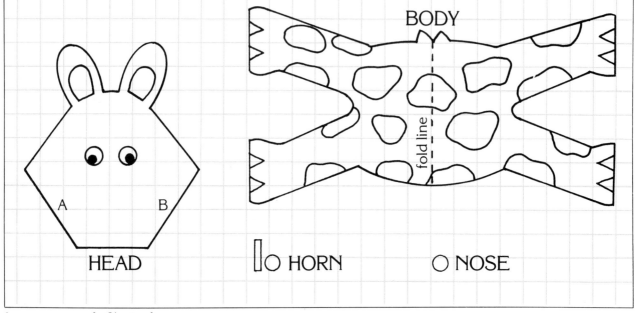

HEAD   A   B

BODY   fold line

HORN   NOSE

1 square equals ⁶/₁₆ inch

32

Newspaper Angel

Materials:

Plastic foam ball 2″ diameter for
   head
Flesh-color acrylic paint
3 sheets newspaper,
   approximately 14″ x 14″
White tacky glue
Gold spray paint
Glitter, fine gold and coarse
   diamond dust
1 yd. gold braid for trim (we used
   self-adhesive)
Black construction paper for
   eyelashes
Red felt for mouth
Blond fake fur 1¼″ x 7″ (see note
   on page 34), or 6 cotton balls,
   for hair
Straight pins
Chatelaine cord with wire center,
   or 1 gold chenille glitter stem,
   for halo

Instructions:

Paint plastic foam ball flesh-
color. Set aside to dry. Glue three
thicknesses of newspaper together. Using patterns on pages
34 and 35 as guide, cut body,
sleeves, wings, and collar. Glue
body together, overlapping in
front ¼ inch to form cone. Glue
sleeves together, overlapping ¼
inch to form cones. Let set. Glue
sleeves in place on sides of body
using photo as guide. Glue *collar*
over top of body and sleeves, overlapping in back. Paint entire body
and sleeves with gold spray paint.
Paint both sides of wings with
gold spray paint. Let dry. Lightly
coat one side of wings with tacky
glue. Sprinkle with coarse diamond dust glitter. Shake off any
excess glitter. Using photo as
guide, lightly coat front of body
with glue and sprinkle with fine
gold glitter. Shake off any excess
glitter. Attach gold braid trim
along edge of collar, sleeves,
skirt, and up front of body, using
photo as guide. Cut two *eyes* from
black construction paper and
mouth from red felt following pat-

tern. Glue eyes and mouth to plastic foam ball as shown in photo.

Brush fur away crosswise from cut edge (Fig. 1). Apply line of glue ¼ inch from edge *on fur side.* Glue and pin *fur side down* around middle of plastic foam ball. Let dry. Fold fur strip back along glue line. Comb fur to center top, pull into a bun, and pin and glue in place (see photo). (If you are using cotton balls for hair, glue cotton balls to head, stretching to cover entire hair surface.) *To attach head to body,* poke hole in bottom of plastic foam head approximately ½ inch in diameter, ½ inch in depth. Dip tip of collar in glue and insert into hole in plastic foam ball. Let dry. Form 1½-inch-diameter *halo* from chatelaine cord or glitter stem, leaving approximately 1½-inch stem (Fig. 2). Insert stem into back center of head and bend halo up and over the top of head as shown in photo. Glue wings to back of body ¾ inch down from neckline.

Note: To cut fur, fold it skin up. Mark 1¼ inches, then with single-edged razor blade, cut carefully through skin only. Repeat for 7-inch measurement, again cutting through skin only.

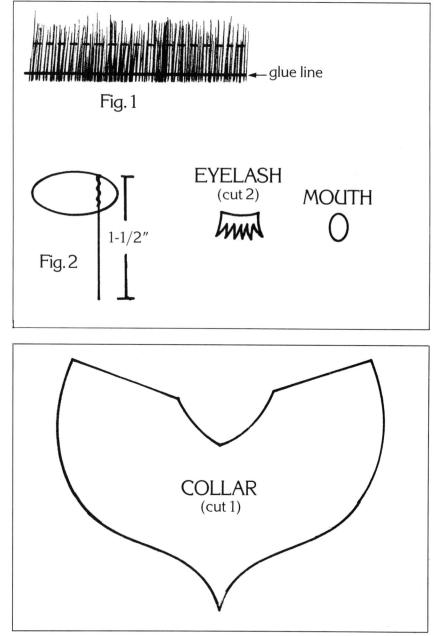

glue line

Fig. 1

Fig. 2

1-1/2"

EYELASH
(cut 2)

MOUTH

COLLAR
(cut 1)

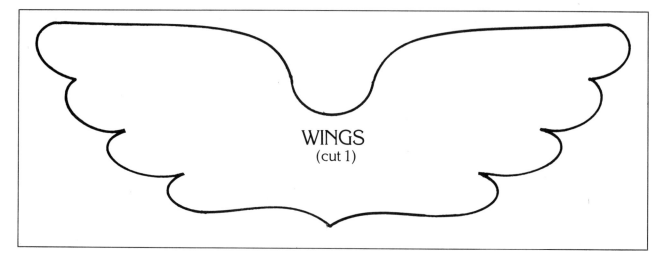

WINGS
(cut 1)

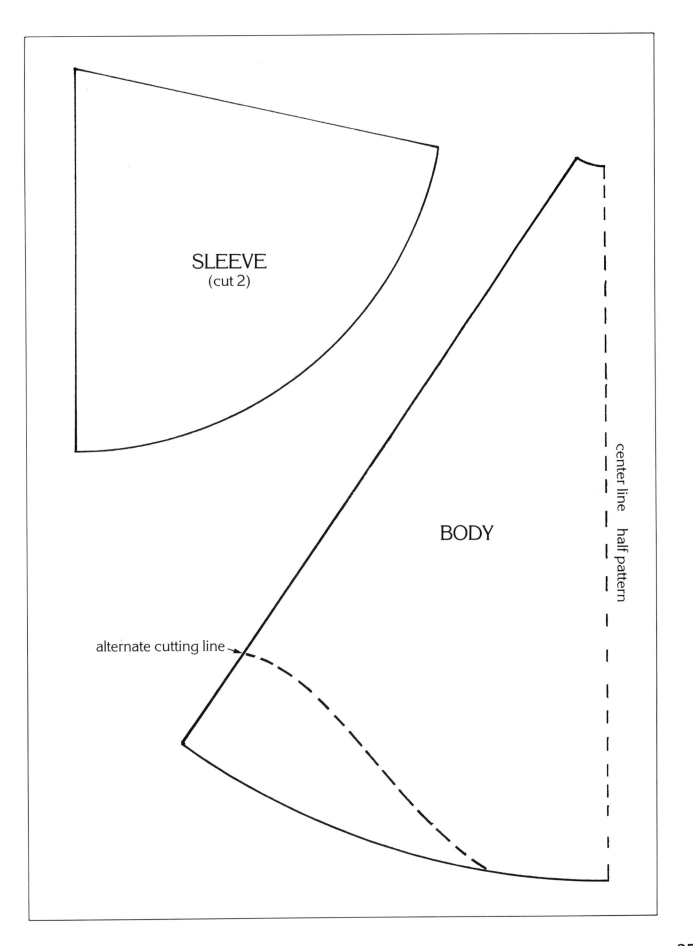

SLEEVE
(cut 2)

BODY

center line   half pattern

alternate cutting line

35

Jewelry from Newspaper

Materials:

Newspaper
White tacky glue
Pin backs for pins
Jump rings for necklaces
Acrylic paint: white and other
  colors
Permanent fine-line black
  marking pen
Spray or brush-on varnish or
  glaze

Instructions:

For all shapes, glue four thicknesses of newspaper together with tacky glue. Be certain that you use tacky glue—it is flexible when dry which allows you to shape the design, if necessary, and to prevent cracking after drying. To achieve a smooth gluing job, spread glue evenly onto single thickness of newspaper. Use your finger or a brush. Place a sheet of newspaper on top of glued sheet. Again, spread an even coat of glue on that sheet and place a sheet of newspaper on top. Repeat until you have the four thicknesses of newspaper glued together. After allowing glue to set approximately twenty minutes, while newspaper is still damp, cut out shape desired. Follow patterns provided or design your own simple shapes. If you are making a design that needs to be shaped (for instance, lips, butterfly wings), you will need to form it at this time while newspaper is still damp. Continue shaping with fingers until design holds shape.

To attach pin backs, apply glue to pin back. Place onto back of newspaper design. Cut a small strip of newspaper and glue over the pin back to secure (paper to paper makes a better bond than metal to paper). *For necklace,* make pin hole for a jump ring. Let design dry overnight. *To paint,* it is best to first give all pieces an undercoat of white paint. This step helps brighten the base color(s). After white undercoat is dry, apply base coat color. To paint flower designs on newspaper shape, dip a toothpick into paint and dot on the flowers. Let dry completely. The black outline or small black dots on design have been drawn on with a fine-line permanent marker. *To finish,* apply varnish or glaze. Test first to make sure that your glaze or varnish is compatible with the marking pen, or lines may run.

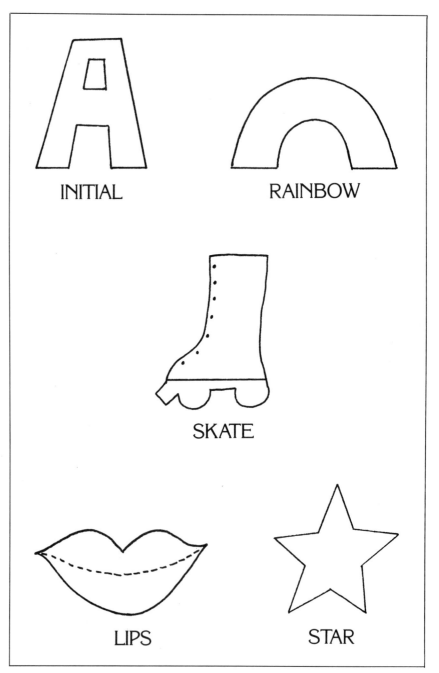

INITIAL

RAINBOW

SKATE

LIPS

STAR

Tissue Painting— Fish on a Basket

Flashing with good humor, these fish think they're pretty special, and they are. A clever offshoot of tissue collage, this new technique will serve you well any time you need to create a hand-painted look quickly and economically.

Materials:

1 new or used wastebasket
Tissue paper: light blue, royal blue, turquoise, lavender, purple, and light pink for fish; light and dark green for seaweed
White matte spray paint
Clear glue (brush-on type)
Soft brush for applying glue
Permanent fine-line black marking pen

Instructions:

Paint wastebasket with white spray paint, covering entire surface. Lightly trace pattern onto paper to transfer to wastebasket. Center pattern and lightly mark key points on wastebasket before gluing down tissue, as you cannot move tissue once it is placed. Be certain to mark lightly, as any heavy pencil marks will show through tissue. Cut front half of fish body from light blue tissue. Tear strips approximately 1½ inches in width from five remaining fish colors to cover remaining fish pattern. (Torn pieces lie better than cut ones.) Tear fin shapes from any color(s) tissue to fit pattern. Tear light and dark green strips for seaweed. Strips of tissue do not have to fit pattern exactly, as shape will be defined with

marking pen when completed.

Brush clear glue onto wastebasket where tissue will be placed. Press light blue tissue in place and apply a coat of clear glue by brushing it over tissue. Repeat process until all tissue strips have been glued in place, filling in body and fins. Glue seaweed strips in place using pattern as guide. Note that seaweed strips have been folded at varying heights to give appearance of movement. Cover entire wastebasket surface with a final coat of clear glue as a sealer. Let dry completely. Using pattern as guide, outline and detail fish and seaweed with permanent fine-line marking pen.

Tissue Painting on Cartons

Materials:

Small plastic juice carton or
    quart milk carton (cut to
    desired height)
White acrylic paint
Tissue paper in various colors
Clear glue
Soft brush
Rickrack for trim (optional)

Instructions:

Cut carton to desired shape and
height. Paint outside. Let dry.
Plan your design and sketch pattern onto carton, or make a free-
form design. Cut desired shapes
from different colors of paper.
Brush clear glue on carton and
lay tissue in place, then brush
clear glue over tissue. Continue
same procedure until pattern is
completed. Glue rickrack trim to
edge, if desired. Coat entire surface with clear glue as a sealer.
Let dry.

CHAPTER THREE

Magic with Scrap Metal and Wood

Few of the projects given in this book require great proficiency with tools—simply the ability to follow easy directions. Well within anyone's ability and strength are the designs using small metals which every household always has—broken zippers and odd keys.

The wood items do not require carpentry skills. Most of our handsome little designs are from the mass-produced throwaways that litter our parks and streets. Using such common junk as burned matches, Popsicle sticks, and thread spools (now largely replaced by plastic spools which function just as well for our craft purposes), we have designed a gallery of gifts, decorative ornaments, salable bazaar items, and toys to be made for and by children. And now wouldn't you—wood you?—like to get started?

Key Wind Chimes

Materials:

1 piece driftwood
Drill
Approximately 12′ clear fishing line
50-100 assorted old keys
Enamel paint (optional)
Approximately 10 beads ⅛″ diameter
White tacky glue
Eye hook for hanger

Instructions:

Drill holes into driftwood at 2-inch intervals with small bit. Cut fishing line into 18-inch lengths (or longer, if desired). Thread one strand of line through hole in first key, leaving a 4-inch excess for tying string to driftwood. Double-knot line to key. Tie a second key below first so that the tip of the first key hits the second key. Continue to desired length of strand.

Repeat the process for all strands. *To attach keys to driftwood,* thread lines through drilled holes. To secure lines, thread through a bead and tie a double knot. Apply a dab of glue to knot and let dry. Cut off excess line above knot. Find center balance point of driftwood and screw eye hook into top at that point for hanger.

Zipper Butterfly

Would you believe it? Something you can make with a broken zipper!

Materials:

1 zipper, 12″ or longer
3″ square scrap art paper or rice paper
White tacky glue
Straight pins

Instructions:

Cut away the cloth that holds zipper teeth. Laying out the zipper on the pattern, cut lengths of teeth to fit. Trace pattern lightly onto art or rice paper. Place paper on a magazine, and glue zipper teeth in place. Hold zipper down with straight pins while glue is drying. When dry, cut away excess paper from outside edge of butterfly.

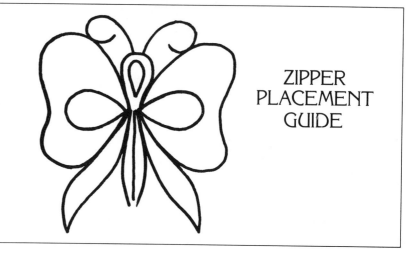

ZIPPER PLACEMENT GUIDE

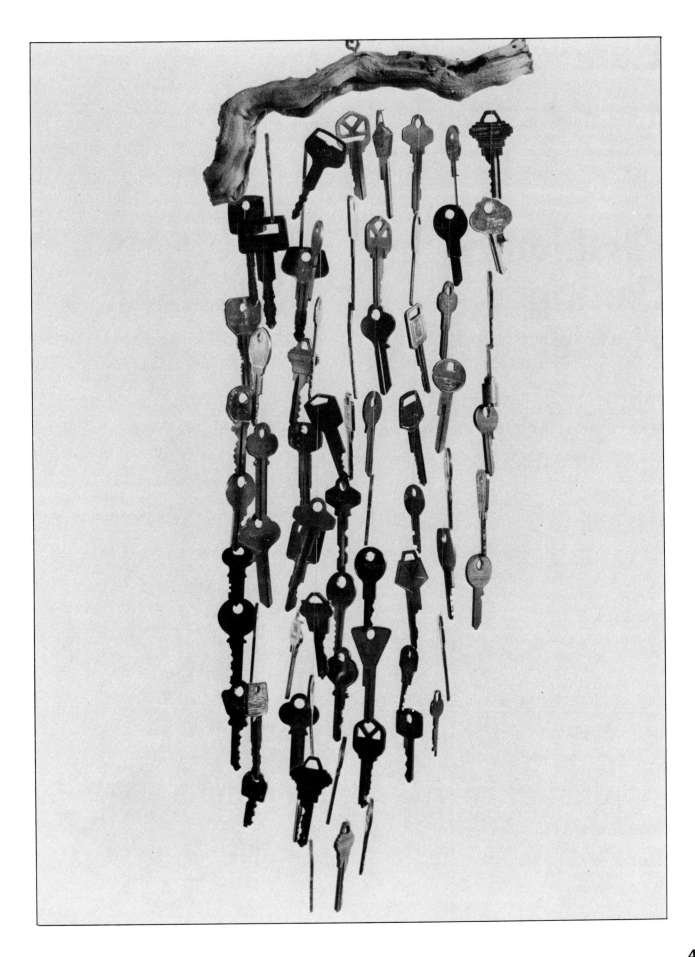

Candleholders

Turn your creative eye on plumbing and electrical supplies—not the usual craft materials—and see them in a new light! We made these candleholders by spray-painting a porcelain light receptacle (and adding hand-painted details), and gluing a stack of conduit connectors with hot glue. Washers and nuts are other design possibilities.

Cushion-Spring Earring Holder

Corkscrew shapes are natural attention-getters, and this one is no exception. We've made a fabric cover for ours, but you might prefer simply to use spray paint.

Materials:

1 cushion spring
Acrylic paint to match fabric
Fabric scraps
Optional trimmings: silk flowers, dried baby's breath, or ribbon

Instructions:

Paint bottom two spirals of spring with acrylic paint for base (see photo). Set aside to dry. Cut strip of fabric 1 inch wide and two times the length of spring coil. (Lay a piece of cord all along the spring, then measure the cord.) Fold strip of fabric in half lengthwise, right sides together, and sew to form tube. Seam allowance will have to be adjusted depending on width of coil, so measure for sewing line. Turn tube right side out and slip onto spring. Push entire length of fabric onto spring, gathering to take up excess. Glue ends of fabric in place at top and bottom. Trim earring holder with silk or dried flowers, or perhaps a bow.

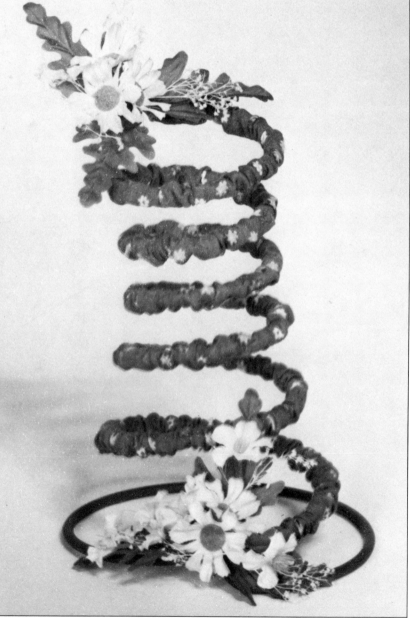

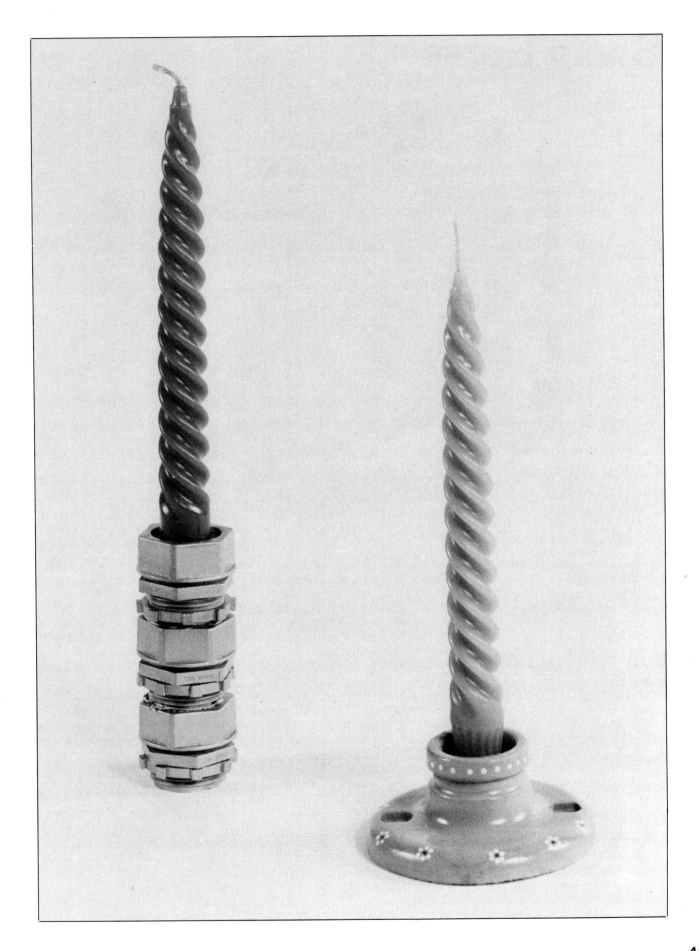

Spool Horse

Materials:

1 large wooden spool about 3″ high

1 wooden spool about 1½″ high

Acrylic paint: light brown, white, and black

Lightweight cardboard

Felt scraps: light brown, hot pink, medium pink, and red

1 chenille stem

White tacky glue

14″ length ⅛″-wide brown satin ribbon

Instructions:

Paint both spools light brown. Set aside to dry. Cut cardboard *rocker* following pattern. Glue a piece of light brown felt to each side of cardboard and cut to cardboard shape. Glue rocker over large spool. Set on side to dry. (To help hold together while drying, wrap with a rubber band.) Cut one circle from light brown felt to cover end of small spool. Glue circle to end. Cut *ears* from light brown felt, using pattern as guide, adjusting pattern to fit your spool. Glue ears onto uncovered end of small spool. Punch a hole through felt into hole in spool with scissor tip. Make a bend in the chenille stem, 1 inch from end. Insert 1 inch into hole in large spool. Glue in place. Let dry. Cut one circle from light brown felt to cover end of large spool. Glue circle to end of large spool opposite chenille stem.

Cut *neck and mane* from light brown felt, using pattern as guide. Glue neck together, with mane in seam, forming a tube shape. Slip neck onto chenille stem, which is now glued to large spool. Slip free end of chenille stem 1 inch through hole punched through felt ear piece. Glue in place to hold. Glue ends of neck to ends of large and small spools. Cut *saddle pad* from medium pink felt, using pattern as guide. Glue in place on top of rocker on large spool. Trim saddle with circles of hot pink felt as shown in photo. Cut ten small hearts from red felt and glue five to each outside length of rocker. Cut *tail* from two thicknesses of light brown felt that have been glued together, following pattern. Glue tail to back of large spool approximately ¼ inch from top edge. Paint eyes on small spool, using photo as guide for placement. For nostrils, paint two small black dots on felt on front of small spool. *To make bridle*, glue satin ribbon around small spool. *To make reins*, glue ends of a 6-inch length of ribbon to each side of head at bridle. Tie ends of reins in bow and glue to saddle or leave hanging around horse's neck.

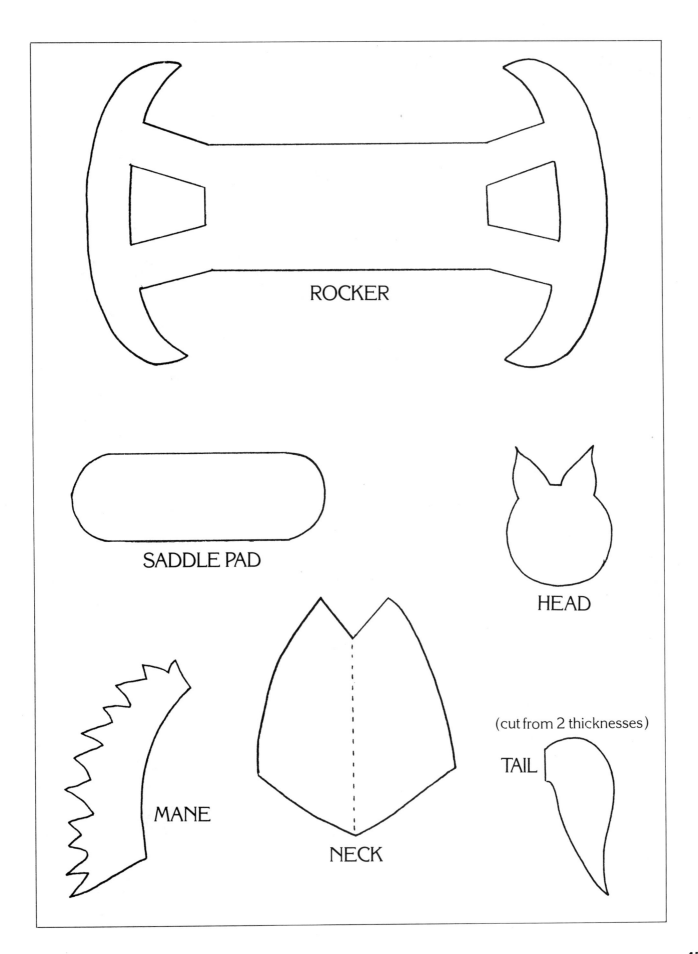

ROCKER

SADDLE PAD

HEAD

MANE

NECK

(cut from 2 thicknesses)

TAIL

Spool Train

Materials:

2 wooden spools about 2½″ high
3 wooden spools about 1¾″ high
Child's wooden building block,
    1¼″ square
Lightweight cardboard scrap
    (about 2″ square)
Acrylic paint: black, purple,
    lavender, blue, white, green,
    and yellow
White tacky glue
1 green wooden bead ⅜″
    diameter
1 red wooden bead ½″ diameter
Purple felt

Instructions:

Paint one large and two small spools black. Paint one large spool blue with lavender around top and bottom edges. Paint one small spool lavender with purple around top and bottom edges.

Paint block green. Using drawing as guide, glue spools and block together. Let dry. Cut out cowcatcher from cardboard, using pattern as guide. Paint black. Let dry. Fold where indicated and glue in front of train. Glue green bead in place behind smokestack.

Glue red bead in middle front of large spool, as shown. Using pattern as guide, cut felt pieces for cab and glue in place on wooden block. Add detail to train by dipping end of toothpick in paint and dotting paint on, using drawing as guide.

Spool Girl

Materials:

2 large wooden spools, each
    about 2″ high, for body
White tacky glue
1 wooden bead 1½″ diameter,
    painted flesh-color, for head
Lightweight cardboard
Acrylic paint: we've used light
    blue, navy blue, ivory, brown,
    flesh-color, green, pink, red,
    and black

Instructions:

Glue the two spools together, one on top of the other. Glue wooden bead on top. Let dry. Cut two arms from cardboard, using pattern as guide. Paint both sides of arms with acrylic paints, to match dress color. Paint hands either white for gloves or flesh-color. Cut hat from cardboard, using pattern as guide. Glue to top of wooden bead at an angle. Let dry. Paint girl and hat, using photo as guide, or create your own design. Glue arms in place on sides of spool.

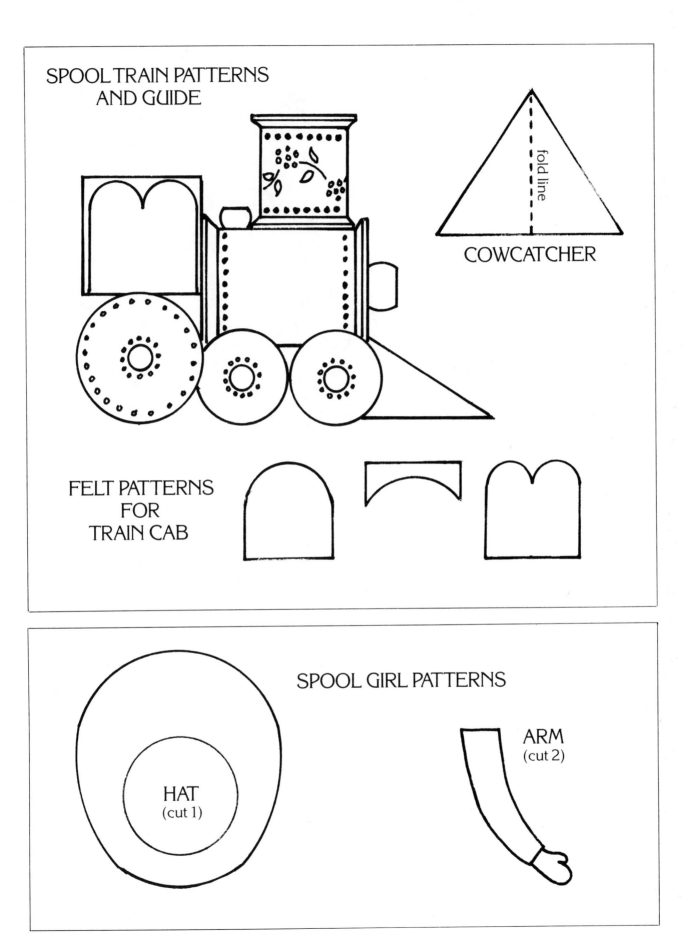

SPOOL TRAIN PATTERNS
AND GUIDE

COWCATCHER

fold line

FELT PATTERNS
FOR
TRAIN CAB

SPOOL GIRL PATTERNS

HAT
(cut 1)

ARM
(cut 2)

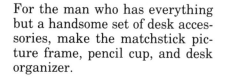

For the man who has everything but a handsome set of desk accessories, make the matchstick picture frame, pencil cup, and desk organizer.

Matchstick Picture Frame

Materials:

Mat board picture frame 8½″ x 9½″
210 burned wooden matchsticks about 2¼″ long (see note)
White tacky glue
Clear acrylic spray varnish sealer
Brown spray paint or antiquing spray (optional)
Soft cloth for use with spray
Gold antiquing paste (optional)

Instructions:

Glue matchsticks in place along sides of frame, then along top and bottom edges, alternating as shown. Let dry. If matchsticks are to be left natural, spray with several coats of varnish sealer. Or, if desired, spray entire surface with brown spray paint or brown antiquing spray and immediately wipe with soft cloth to give matches an antiqued look. Let dry. Highlight with gold antiquing paste, by dabbing finger in paste and lightly spreading it on matchstick surfaces. Let dry. Spray with several coats of sealer.

Note: If you can't wait to accumulate the used matchsticks required for these projects, you can burn them *en masse,* but work outdoors, away from other flammable objects, and provide yourself with a pail of water for dousing the flames. Here's one method: Pile the matches, *heads up,* into a nonburnable container at least half an inch shallower than the length of the matches. With a lighted candle about 16 inches long (so you're not too close to the flame), quickly ignite all of the matches, then douse the flames immediately with water from the pail and lay the sticks flat on the table to dry.

Matchstick Pencil Cup

Materials:

150 burned wooden matchsticks about 2¼" long (see note page 50)

Frozen juice container 4½" high

White tacky glue

Clear acrylic spray varnish sealer

Brown spray paint or antiquing spray (optional)

Gold antiquing paste

Soft cloth for use with spray

Black felt scraps

Instructions:

Glue two rows of matchsticks on outside of container, one end up, second down, continuing this way all around the container in two layers (see photo). Let dry. If matchsticks are to be left natural, spray with several coats of varnish sealer. Or, if desired, spray entire surface with brown spray paint or brown antiquing spray and immediately wipe off with soft cloth to give matches an antiqued look. Let dry. Highlight with gold antiquing paste by dabbing finger in paste and lightly touching matchstick surfaces. Let dry. Spray with several coats of sealer. Glue circle of black felt to bottom of cup and line inside with felt.

Matchstick Desk Organizer

Materials:

Cardboard tissue box

Masking tape

Black acrylic paint or spray paint

200 burned wooden matchsticks (see note page 50)

White tacky glue

4 wooden beads ⅝" diameter for legs

Clear acrylic spray varnish sealer

Brown spray paint or antiquing spray (optional)

Soft cloth for use with spray

Gold antiquing paste (optional)

Instructions:

Cut off top of tissue box and save. Cut box in half lengthwise. Fit halves one inside the other. Tape together with masking tape and cover all edges with masking tape to finish. Cut two 1¾-inch x 2½-inch inserts from the tissue box top to fit inside organizer as the dividers. Tape in place 3¼ inches from ends, forming three compartments. Tape top edges of dividers also, to finish off edges. Spray or paint entire box. Let dry. Glue matchsticks to outside of box, alternating ends of matchsticks. Glue wooden beads on bottom of box, one in each corner, for legs. If matchsticks are to be left natural, spray with several coats of varnish sealer. Or, if desired, spray entire matchstick surface carefully with brown spray paint or brown antiquing spray and immediately wipe off with soft cloth to give matches an antiqued look. Let dry. Highlight with gold antiquing paste, by dabbing finger in paste and lightly touching matchstick surface. Let dry. Spray with several coats of sealer.

Matchstick Christmas Tree

Materials:

9″ x 12″ piece cardboard (shirt size)
1 toilet tissue tube
White tacky glue
Black acrylic paint or spray paint
240 burned wooden matchsticks (see note page 50)
1 wooden bead 1⅝″ diameter
Clear acrylic spray varnish sealer
Brown spray paint or antiquing spray (optional)
Soft cloth (for use with spray)
Gold antiquing paste (optional)

Instructions:

Cut cardboard using pattern as guide. Glue cardboard into cone shape. Let dry. Set cone over toilet tissue tube as shown in photo and glue in place. Let dry. Paint entire outside and underside surface of tree with black paint. Let dry. Starting with toilet tissue base, glue matchsticks around base, burned ends facing down. Next, start gluing matches at bottom of cone, extending burned end approximately ½ inch below bottom of cone. Glue next row of matchsticks on cone overlapping first row approximately 1 inch. Repeat two more times. For top of tree, cut and taper ½ inch off ten matchsticks. Alternate cut matches with whole matchsticks to fill in as shown in photo. Glue wooden bead to top of cone. If matchsticks are to be left natural, spray with several coats of varnish sealer. Or, if desired, spray entire surface with brown spray paint or brown antiquing spray and immediately wipe off with soft cloth to give matches an antiqued look. Let dry. Highlight with gold antiquing paste, by dabbing finger in paste and lightly touching matchstick surface. Let dry. Spray with several coats of sealer.

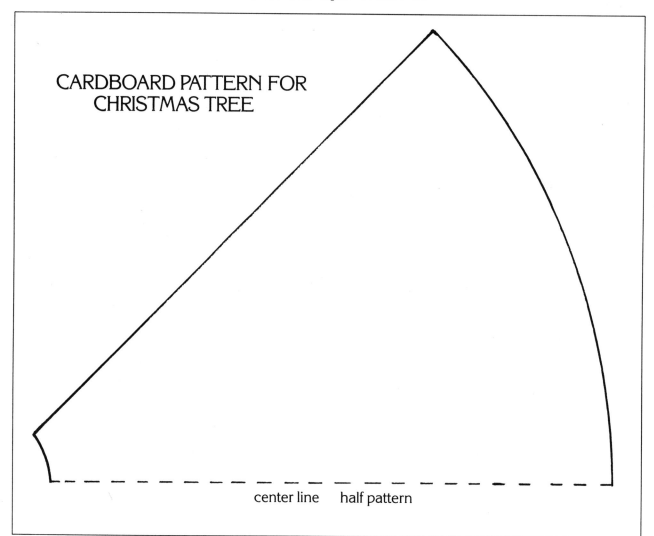

CARDBOARD PATTERN FOR CHRISTMAS TREE

center line   half pattern

The minimum cost and the speed
with which it can be made, plus
its maximum appeal, make this a
fine fund-raising project.

Popsicle Stick Angel

Materials:

30" white yarn for hair
1 wooden bead ⅝" diameter for head
3" piece 22-gauge wire or white chenille stem
Permanent fine-line black marking pen (other colors optional)
5 Popsicle sticks for body and wings
Wire cutters
White tacky glue
White acrylic paint (other colors optional)
Fine diamond-dust glitter (optional)
Spray glue (optional)
Gold cord for hanger (optional)

Instructions:

Make angel's *head* from yarn, bead, and chenille stem or wire, following instructions for Angels from Doilies, page 22. Draw eyes, nose, and mouth on bead with the marking pen, as shown in photo. To make *wings*, cut two Popsicle sticks with wire cutters, patterns A and B. For *body*, use three whole Popsicle sticks, following pattern for placement. Glue in place. Let dry. Paint body with white acrylic paint. Let dry. Angel may be decorated with paint, marking pens, etc. Or body may be sprayed with spray glue and dusted with glitter. Glue head in place between wings, attaching wire or chenille stem neck to back or body by gluing. Attach hanger with glue, if desired.

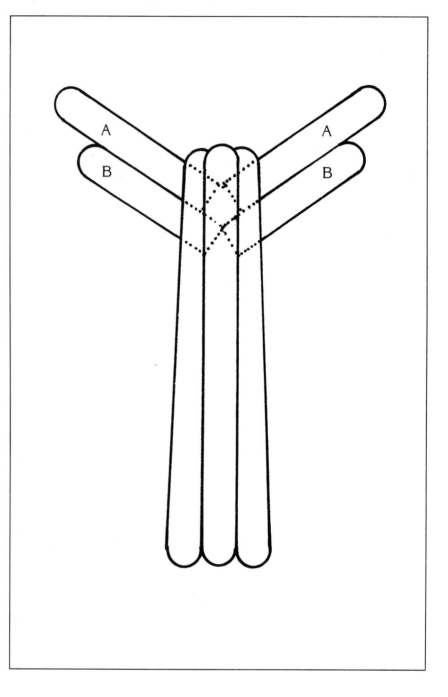

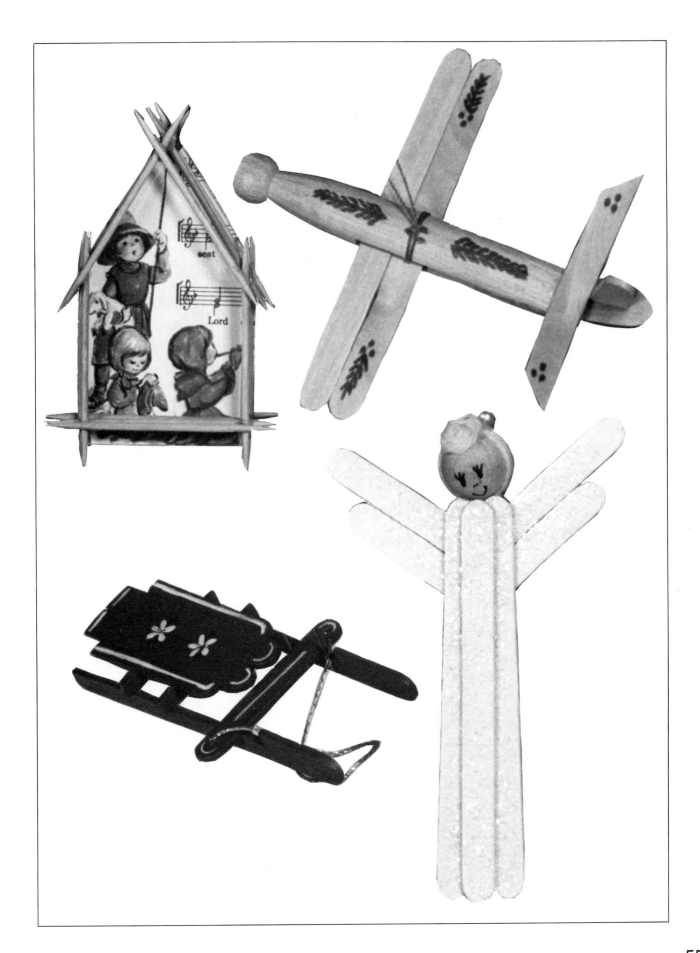

Popsicle Stick Airplane

(See photo on page 55.)

Materials:

2 old-fashioned wooden
    clothespins
White tacky glue
3 Popsicle sticks
2 wooden beads approximately
    ½″ diameter
Wire cutters
Optional trimmings: various
    colors acrylic paints or
    permanent marking pens and
    glitter
Gold cord for hanger (optional)

Instructions:

To make airplane's wings, glue
two Popsicle sticks at top of slot
in clothespin, Fig. 1. For wheels,
glue the two wooden beads on
sides of clothespin body, Fig. 2. *To
make tail section,* cut a 1¼-inch
section from second clothespin (A)
with wire cutters, and two Popsi-

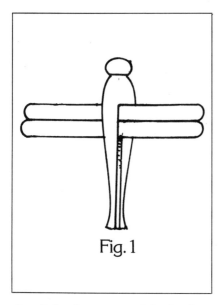

Fig. 1

cle stick pieces: one 1-inch piece
cut at angle (B) and one 3-inch
piece angled at both ends (C). Assemble airplane following drawing as guide, and glue in place.
For airplane detail, decorate with
acrylic paint or marking pens and
glitter, as desired. Tie on gold
cord for hanger, if desired.

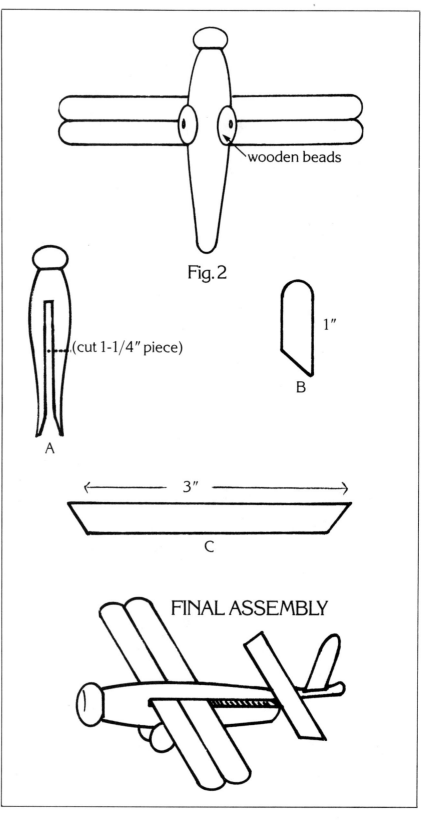

wooden beads

Fig. 2

(cut 1-1/4″ piece)

A

B

1″

3″

C

FINAL ASSEMBLY

Popsicle Sled

(See photo on page 55.)

Materials:

6 Popsicle sticks
Wire cutters
Hammer and nail, or small drill
2 burned wooden matchsticks
White tacky glue
Optional trimmings: various
    colors acrylic paints or
    permanent marking pens,
    fabric scraps, braid
8″ thin gold cord for sled pull

Instructions:

Cut two runners from two Popsicle sticks following drawing as a guide. Cut pieces A, B, and C following pattern. Use hammer and nail or small drill to punch holes in A to attach cord. Glue piece A in place on runners, using drawings as guide. Cut tips from two matchsticks. Glue in place across runners as shown. Let dry. Glue pieces B (two) and C (two) in place on matchsticks. Let dry. Decorate with acrylic paints or felt markers, or trim with fabric and braids, if desired. Attach gold cord to piece A.

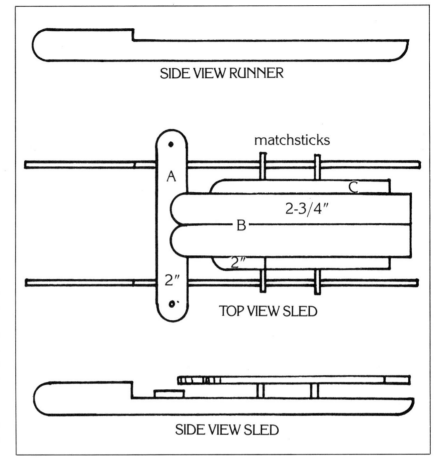

Toothpick Niche

(See photo on page 55.)

Everyone finds this toothpick project fun to do. It's simple enough for the very young, and can be professional-looking so it interests the older craftsman as well.

Materials:

20 wooden toothpicks
White tacky glue
Christmas or other greeting card
    with picture approximately 3″
    square for background
8″ gold cord for hanger

Instructions:

To make niche, glue five toothpicks together using drawing as guide to form base. Lay vertical toothpicks down first and glue three remaining toothpicks on top. Let dry. Cut card to size to fit niche. Glue card in place over base. Let dry. Continue to layer toothpicks following pattern, creating three layers. Let dry. Tie hanger at top through toothpicks.

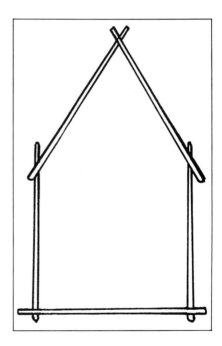

Clothespin Drum Major

Materials:

1 old-fashioned clothespin
Acrylic paint: black, white, green, red, and pink
1 black cloth pom-pom 1½" diameter for hat
White tacky glue
6" narrow gold braid for leg and chin strap
2" strip ¾" black electrical tape
2 burned wooden matchsticks for arms
Glitter or sequins for buttons
⅓ yd. thin gold cord for hanger (optional)

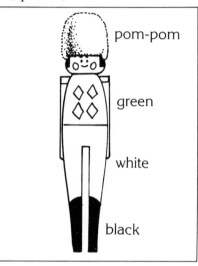

pom-pom

green

white

black

Instructions:

For drum major's body, paint the bottom ¼ inch of clothespin black for shoes. Paint the next 2 inches of clothespin white for the pants. Paint the remainder of the body up to neckline green for the coat. Using drawing as guide, paint hair black, leaving face natural. Paint black circles with white dots for eyes, a black dot for nose, and a red half circle for mouth. For cheeks, paint two large dots with pink paint. To make *arms,* cut off tips of matchsticks and paint the sticks green with white tips, representing gloved hands. For *hat,* glue black pom-pom on the top of the head. Cut the gold trim into three 2-inch pieces. Glue one piece of trim on each side of clothespin for pants trim. Glue the remaining piece under chin up to each side of hat for the chin strap. For *cummerbund,* wrap black tape around waist, overlapping in back. Glue matchstick arms to sides of clothespin, ⅛ inch down from neckline. For *buttons,* glue glitter or sequins to coat front as shown in drawing. If desired, glue hanger to hat.

CLOTHESPIN FIGURES

There was a time when Papa or Grandpapa painstakingly whittled small dolls and toys, starting with a single block of wood and carving slowly and carefully until each feature could pass his critical inspection. These handcrafted toys—now, alas, mostly a thing of the past—are highly treasured by collectors. Since we can't restore the old crafts or bring back the patient craftsman, we've done the next best thing for busy people who still want a touch of themselves in objects they make for their children and grandchildren. The old-fashioned wooden clothespin, while obviously not hand-carved, has just the shape needed for stick-figure soldiers, girls, animals, and creatures of the imagination. We've given you a few designs (and photographed a few others) to get you started on building your own menagerie and doll collection for the little ones of your family.

If you haven't saved those wooden clothespins, look for them in notion and variety stores, in flea markets, and—a popular stock item—wherever craft materials are sold.

Clothespin Soldier

Materials:

1 old-fashioned clothespin for body
Acrylic paint: blue, red, black, and yellow
White tacky glue
1 wooden toothpick, end blunted
1 burned wooden matchstick for arms
1 black cloth pom-pom 1½" diameter for hat
⅓ yd. thin gold cord for hanger (optional)

Instructions:

To make the soldier's body, paint the bottom 2½ inches of clothespin blue for pants. Paint remainder of body to neck red for soldier's coat. Let dry. Paint hair black, leaving face natural. Using blunted tip of toothpick dipped in black paint, dab on two dots for eyes and one for the mouth. Let dry. For soldier's *buttons,* use blunted tip of toothpick dipped in yellow paint and dab on three dots, following photograph. *To*

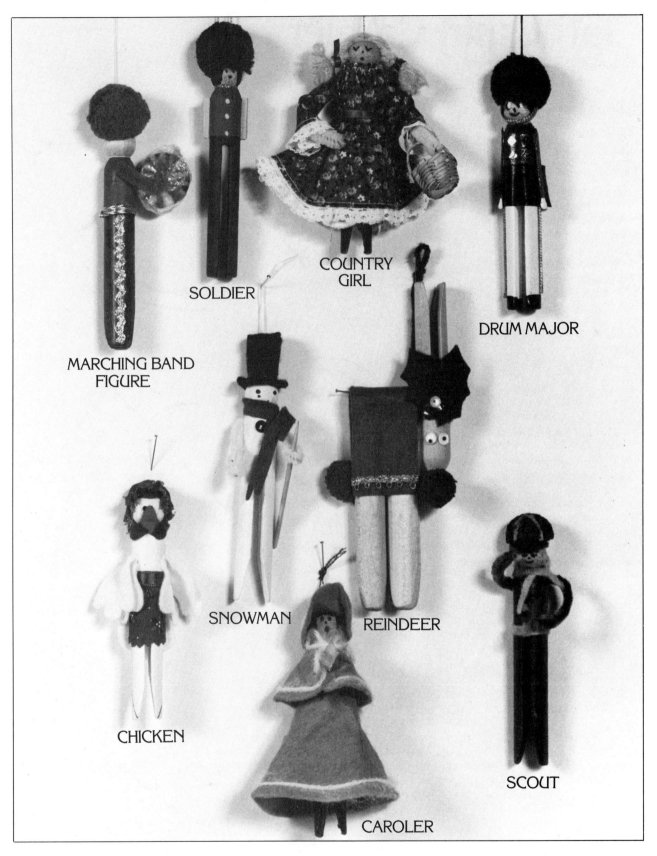

MARCHING BAND
FIGURE

SOLDIER

COUNTRY
GIRL

DRUM MAJOR

SNOWMAN

REINDEER

CHICKEN

SCOUT

CAROLER

make soldier's arms, cut burned tip off matchstick and then cut matchstick in half. Paint both halves yellow. Let dry. Glue arms in place on sides of clothespin. For *hat,* glue pom-pom to top of clothespin. If desired, tie gold cord around soldier's neck for hanger.

Clothespin Caroler

(See photo on page 59.)

Materials:

1 old-fashioned clothespin for body
Acrylic paint: black, white, and brown
Permanent fine-line black and red marking pens
White tacky glue
Felt 9" x 11" for dress, cape, and hat
⅔ yd. yarn for trim
Gold cardboard for book
⅓ yd. thin gold cord for hanger (optional)

Instructions:

For caroler's body, paint bottom ½ inch of clothespin black for shoes. Paint remaining body white up to neckline. Leave face natural. *For face features,* use permanent fine-line marking pens, black for eyes and nose and red for mouth. Paint hair brown, following drawing. Trace *skirt, cape, and hat* patterns on felt and cut. Glue yarn in place on each piece, following pattern guide. Glue skirt to body ½ inch down from neckline, overlapping ¼ inch to form cone shape. Glue seam together. Glue cape to body at neck, overlapping in front ¼ inch to form cone shape. Glue seam together. Tie bow from yarn, glue to front of caroler ¼ inch down from neckline. *To make book,* cut gold cardboard ½ inch x 1 inch. Fold in half lengthwise. Glue lengthwise edge of book to front of cape using photograph as guide. *For caroler's hat,* overlap V-cut edge ¼ inch and glue. Glue to head. Tie gold cord around caroler's neck for hanger, if desired.

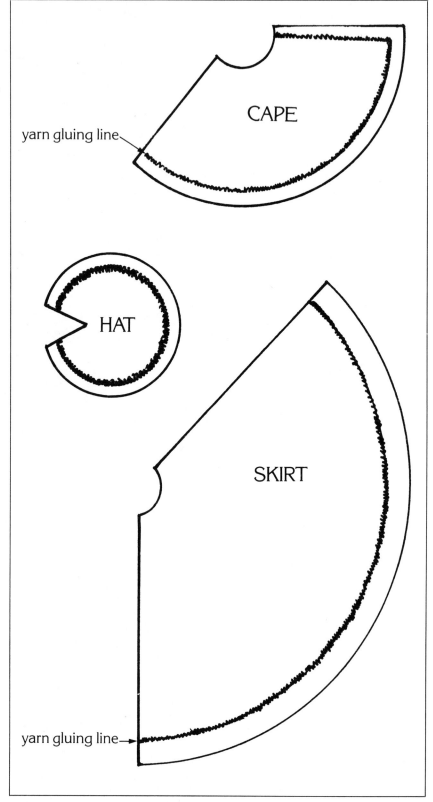

yarn gluing line

CAPE

HAT

SKIRT

yarn gluing line

Clothespin Reindeer

(See photo on page 59.)

Materials:

3 old-fashioned clothespins for
   body and head
White tacky glue
Felt: red for blanket, green for
   leaves
1½″ gold trim for blanket
2 red cloth pom-poms ½″
   diameter for nose and tail
3 red sequins for holly berries
2 moving eyes, 7 mm.
4″ yarn for hanger (optional)

Instructions:

For body of reindeer, glue two clothespins together side by side. Glue the third clothespin upside down, halfway down the other two, forming antlers and head (see drawing). *To make blanket,* cut a 1½ inch x 4 inch strip of red felt. Glue blanket in place by folding in half over the top of the body. Glue 1½ inches of gold trim to front of felt blanket as shown in photograph. *For tail and nose,* using photograph as guide, glue pom-poms on body. Trace two *holly leaves* from pattern onto green felt and cut. Overlapping the leaves at the bottom, glue in place 1¼ inches up from nose as shown in photograph. Glue three sequins at base of leaves for berries. Glue eyes close together halfway between nose and leaves. If hanger is desired, tie yarn around joint between head and body.

HOLLY
LEAF
(cut 2)

Clothespin Snowman

(See photo on page 59.)

Materials:

1 old-fashioned clothespin for
   body
White acrylic paint
Permanent fine-line black and
   red marking pens
1 white chenille stem for arms
White tacky glue
Felt scraps: red for scarf, black
   for hat
Compass to draw hat
2 black sequins
Wooden toothpick, one end
   blunted
⅓ yd. thin gold cord for hanger
   (optional)

Instructions:

For snowman's body, paint entire clothespin white. Let dry. Draw face on with permanent marking pens—black for eyes and nose, red for mouth—using drawing as guide. *To make arms,* cut two lengths of chenille stem, each 1½ inches long. Bend ½ inch of each stem back, forming hands. Glue arms in place on sides of clothespin ¼ inch down for snowman's neckline. *To make snowman's hat,* cut rectangle 2¼ inches x 1¼ inches from black felt. Overlap strip ⅛ inch and glue in place forming cylinder. Glue cylinder to ⅜-inch circle. Glue ½-inch circle on top, forming hat. Glue hat to top of snowman's head. Glue two sequins on front of snowman for buttons. Cut rectangle 4 inches x 1¼ inches for *scarf* from red felt following pattern. Wrap around snowman's neck, overlapping at side. Glue in place. Glue toothpick in one hand of snowman. Tie gold cord around snowman's neck for hanger, if desired.

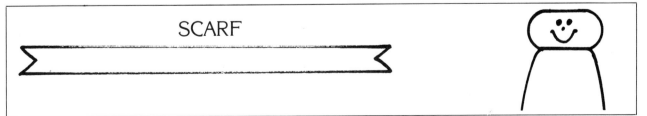

SCARF

Clothespin Chicken

(See photo on page 59.)

Materials:

1 old-fashioned clothespin for
   body
White acrylic paint
Fabric scraps for apron and hat
Compass to draw hat
Pinking shears (optional)
Needle and thread
Felt scraps: red for comb and
   wattles, orange for beak, light
   yellow for feathers
White tacky glue
2 black seed beads for eyes
6" narrow ribbon for apron tie
⅓ yd. thin gold cord for hanger
   (optional)

Instructions:

For chicken's body, paint clothespin white. Let dry. Cut *comb* from red felt, using pattern as guide. Fold where indicated and glue on top of clothespin. *For eyes,* glue two beads in middle of face as shown in photograph. *To make chicken's hat,* cut circle 1½ inch in diameter from fabric scraps. Edge of fabric may be cut with pinking shears to add detail and prevent fraying.) Gather circle to fit top of clothespin by sewing a basting stitch ¼ inch in from edge of fabric. Stuff hat with cotton or felt or fabric scraps to keep it from collapsing. Attach hat to head with glue. Cut *beak* from orange felt, using pattern as guide. Fold where indicated and glue beak to head at neckline beneath eyes. Cut *wattles* from red felt, using pattern as guide. Glue in place underneath beak, using photograph as guide. Cut *apron* from fabric scraps, using pattern as guide. (Edge of fabric may be cut with pinking shears to add detail and to prevent fraying.) Glue apron 1 inch down on front of chicken. Glue ribbon around waistline, covering top raw edge of apron. Tie bow in back. Cut three *feathers* from light yellow felt, using pattern as guide. Fold where indicated and glue one on each side of chicken for wings, using photograph as guide. Glue remaining feather on back side of chicken, under bow, for tail. Tie gold cord around chicken's neck for hanger, if desired.

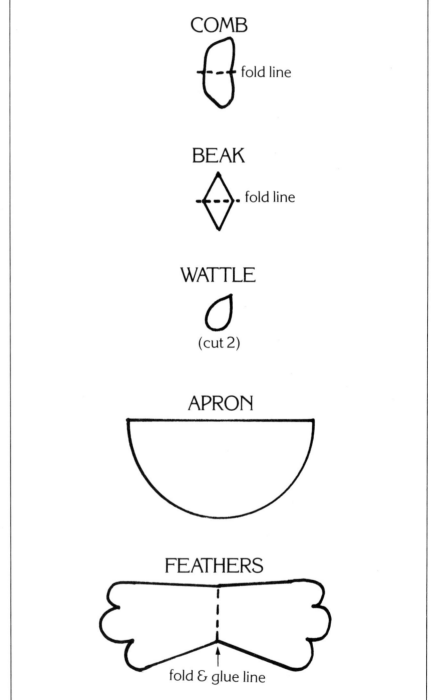

COMB

fold line

BEAK

fold line

WATTLE

(cut 2)

APRON

FEATHERS

fold & glue line

CHAPTER FOUR
Fun with Food

Here's a potpourri of designs for nimble fingers
using pantry items that you might not have
realized would lend themselves to craft projects.
Walnuts, pretzels, peanuts, cereal, and other
nonspoilable pantry-shelf edibles, when sprayed
with a glaze, can be used in making long-lasting
ornaments. Bread dough can be molded like clay
and used in many surprising and creative ways. So
open the cupboard and get started!

Licorice Picture Frames

A candy-store goodie makes a pretty frame for a get-well card to carry to a convalescent. Youngsters will like it too.

Materials:

Greeting card
Cardboard cut to same size as
    card
White tacky glue
Licorice sticks
Gold antiquing paste
Spray varnish sealer
Soft-margarine container lid for
    frame (optional)
Acrylic paint (optional)

Instructions:

Glue greeting card to cardboard. Glue licorice around edge of card. The licorice can be cut on an angle to miter corners, if desired. Let dry. Antique the licorice with gold antiquing paste by dabbing finger in paste, removing excess on a paper towel, then lightly rubbing finger on ridges of licorice. Seal licorice and surface of card by spraying with several coats of spray varnish sealer. Let dry completely between each coat.

For a round frame, use a soft margarine container lid. Spray or paint lid in a color to coordinate or contrast with card. Cut card to fit center and glue in place. Let dry. Glue licorice around inside of lid. Let dry. Paint licorice, if desired, and antique it. Spray entire picture and frame with several coats of spray sealer. Let dry between each coat.

Owl Wall Hanging

Let your imagination run wild and create zany wall hangings that are sure to be conversation pieces. (Our owls are made of pretzels, Cheerios, and walnut shells.) Turn the kids loose and see what they can come up with when the table is laden with edibles in all shapes and sizes—ordinary, everyday objects and now they are design materials! That's education! Be sure to supply fabric, paper, or wood backgrounds.

Materials:

16″ x 6″ piece of burlap for
  background
White tacky glue
Dowel stick 7″ long
3 straight pretzels for perches
3 twisted pretzels for heads
9 Cheerios for eyes and feet
3 walnut shell halves for bodies
Spray or brush-on varnish sealer
  (optional)
Fishing line or heavy-duty
  thread for hanger

Instructions:

Fold burlap over 1 inch at top and stitch or glue ⅝ inch from edge. This forms a hem through which you can insert a dowel stick for a hanger. *To fringe,* draw line of glue on back of burlap ½ inch from edge on all three sides. Let dry. Pull threads from cut edge to glue line. If desired, spray the pretzels and Cheerios with a clear acrylic spray or brush on any type of protective glaze. Let dry. Using photograph as guide, lay materials out on burlap to test placement. Then glue on walnut shells, followed by twisted pretzels for heads and straight pretzel for perches. Glue Cheerios in twisted pretzel for eyes. Cut Cheerios in half and glue onto perch for feet. To hang, tie fishing line or heavy-duty thread to dowel.

Peanut Necklace

It's true what they say: Nobody ever stops with just one peanut necklace!

Materials:

About 20 whole peanuts with hole drilled in them (see note)
Drill (see note)
24″ 20-pound-test fishing line (or more for longer necklace)
Spray varnish
26 wooden beads ⅜″ diameter
1 barrel clasp (jewelry finding)
1 silver tube for crimping line (jewelry finding)

Instructions:

Thread drilled nuts onto fishing line and spray all sides with several coats of varnish. String wooden beads onto line and at-tach a barrel clasp according to directions with Bread Dough Fruit Necklace, page 74.

Note: Pick a small drill size and exercise caution if using an electric drill. It's best to mark exact spot for drilling, then secure the nuts in a vise to hold them stationary during the drilling.

Spice Wreath

Lots of spice and everything nice in this circle of fragrance to hang on the wall or Christmas tree. When you tire of the wreath, you can pull off the bay leaves for use (if they haven't been varnished).

Materials:

Large whole dried bay leaves
Brown grocery bag or lightweight cardboard (optional)
White tacky glue
Assorted spices (cloves, cinnamon stick, fennel seed, caraway seed, celery seed, etc.)
Assorted dried beans (optional)
Ribbon for trim (optional)
Paper hole puncher
Spray varnish (optional)
Gold cord for hanger

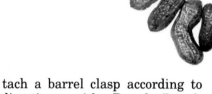

Instructions:

To form casing for ring, pin gether, overlapping to form a circle approximately 4 inches in diameter. For added strength, leaves may be glued to a cardboard or brown bag base. Glue beans and larger spices onto wreath first and work down to the smaller spices. Glue bows on for trim, if desired. Punch hole through bay leaves for hanger. Wreath may be coated with spray varnish or left natural for maximum scent. Tie on gold cord for hanger.

Macaroni Ornaments

You've heard that pasta is *prima* on the party circuit? Now it's a *prima* design material in our book, and to prove that there's more to pasta than just plain spaghetti, we've used the less familiar tube cut on the diagonal in 2½-inch lengths. Other shapes can be substituted, of course.

Macaroni Christmas Tree

Materials:

Cardboard 3″ square
White tacky glue
1-pound package mostaccioli macaroni
Green acrylic paint
Spray glue
Fine diamond-dust glitter
Assorted wooden beads ¼″ diameter for trim
Wire hanger

Instructions:

Cut cardboard tree shape as shown in drawing on page 68, using dotted line as guide. Glue macaroni in place as shown and let dry. Paint green. Let dry. Spray top surface with spray glue and sprinkle with glitter. Using white tacky glue, add wooden beads. Let dry. Glue on hanger.

Macaroni Whimsies

Using the materials and directions given for the tree, follow the designs in the drawings on pages 68–69 or create your own shapes. Glue on loop of gold cord for hanger.

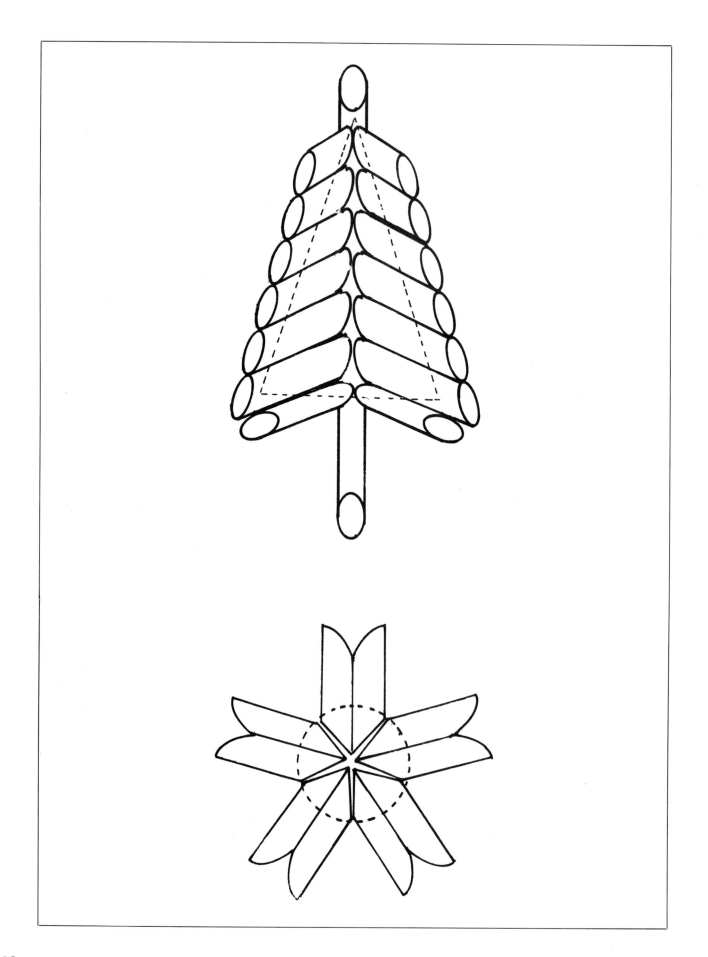

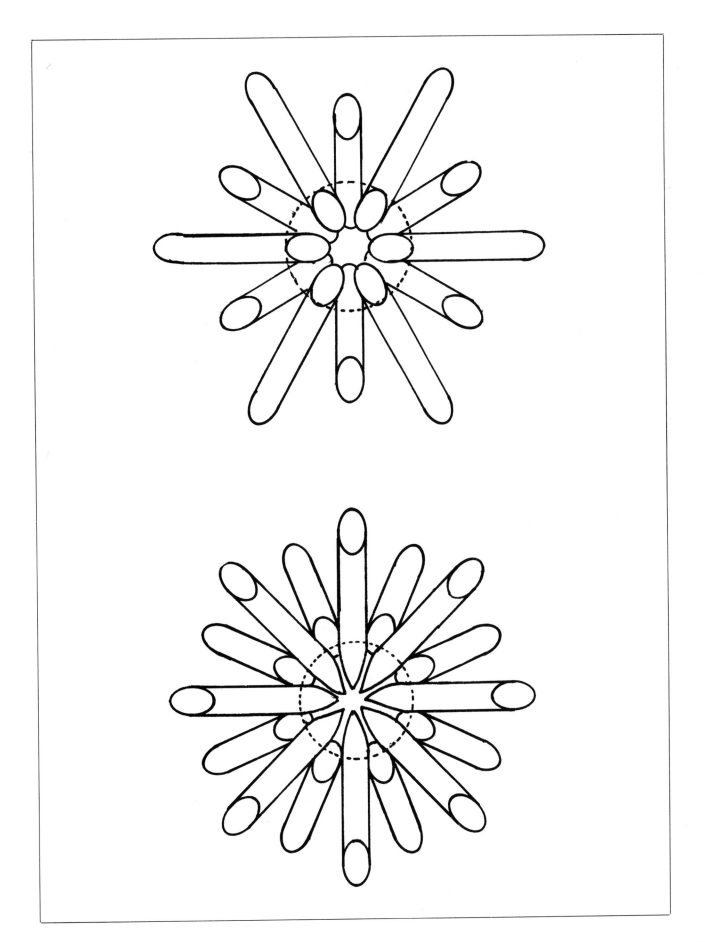

Corn Flake Tree

Here's the good news about stale corn flakes—or other cold cereals, which will work just as well here!

Materials:

1 plastic foam cone, 4″ x 12″
1 plastic foam base, 4″ x 3″
2 wooden toothpicks
White tacky glue
1 box corn flakes
Gold spray paint
Spray glue
Fine gold glitter
6 yds. ¼″ ribbon (we've used 3 yds. red, 3 yds. green)
1 multi-looped bow, 4 loops each side (see instructions page 158)
Dried flowers
45 pearl head pins
45 wooden beads ⅜″ diameter

Instructions:

To make the tree, fasten the large end of the cone to the small end of the base with glue and wooden picks as shown in drawing. Brush glue onto the tree,

small sections at a time. Pick out the large corn flakes. Apply additional glue to the edges of the corn flakes and stick them on the tree, working from the bottom up. Cover the entire tree by overlapping the corn flakes close enough so that no plastic foam shows through. After you have covered the entire tree, go back and fill in any bare spots with more corn flakes. Let dry. Spray the tree with gold spray paint. Let dry. Spray the entire tree with spray glue and immediately sprinkle on the glitter. Glitter the tree quite heavily. Where you need more glitter, respray the glue and sprinkle again with glitter. Gently shake off excess glitter lying in cracks and crevices. Give the entire tree a final spray with the spray glue to hold the glitter firmly.

To decorate the tree, tie small bows from the red and green ribbon. Sixteen bows were used on the tree in the photograph and three were used on the base. Glue bows to side of tree at varied intervals, with five or six dried flowers underneath. Use photograph as guide for placement. Glue multi-looped bow on top of the tree. *For the base,* we have decorated with wooden beads and pins. Simply pin the beads onto the base with the pearl head pins. Three bows have also been glued to base for trim.

Bread Dough Rose Pendant with Matching Earrings and Hair Comb

Bread dough flowers were first made in Mexico, with nine or ten different dough ingredients and with shoe polish added for pliability, but the flowers soon deteriorated and attracted bugs. Our dough recipe is the only one we know of that does not attract bugs. The roses shown, approximately ½ inch in diameter, are painted light and dark pink, but roses come in many different hues, so pick a palette of colors that is most flattering to you.

Materials:

Bread dough (see instructions in box)
Food colors, water colors, tempera, or oil or acrylic paints: light and dark pinks for roses, green for leaves
White tacky glue
Manicure scissors
Straight pin or nail for marking leaves
Pendant and earring mountings
Hair comb
Dried baby's breath and narrow ribbon for trim (optional)

Instructions:

Prepare the dough as directed. You can paint the roses after they are formed, or color the dough now. To add color at this point, shape the dough into three 1-inch balls. Adding a drop or two of color at a time, and mixing it in thoroughly, color one ball light pink, the second ball dark pink,

and the third ball green. (Use acrylics for a more porcelain effect, food coloring for a translucent effect.) Continue until the hues are just what you want. *To make the rose center*, take a piece of bread dough (dark pink, if precolored) about the size of a pea. Press with your thumb and fin-

BREAD DOUGH DESIGNS

Designs made from bread dough are particularly effective, and no modeling medium is quite as versatile. It is easy to mold, inexpensive, and durable, and it dries to look like porcelain. There are many different bread-dough recipes, but the one which follows kneads into a smooth perfect dough, unlike most others which are rough and uneven. This dough can be used in making elegant jewelry, molding dolls' hands and feet, repairing antique picture frames, and in dozens of other ways. Since the glue is plastic-based, not wheat-based, the dough becomes plasticized, which renders it crack-free, bug-free, and quite unbreakable.

Making Bread Dough

To make dough, use 1 slice of soft white bread to 1 tablespoon of white tacky glue (a good amount for one batch: 6 slices bread and 6 tablespoons glue). Remove the crust and using only the white part, tear the bread into tiny pieces. Put the pieces into a container (a paper or plastic cup is good, or a plastic bag). Add the glue. Mix, knead, and squeeze the bread and glue with your hands for approximately five minutes. For the first few minutes, you will have a mess in your hands. Then, like magic, it becomes a dough that no longer sticks to your hands and will have a smooth, even texture. The dough peels off of your hands and rolls into a dough ball. Store the dough in a plastic bag, as it will dry out when exposed to the air. Just take out the amount you need as you work.

gers to flatten pea until it is about as thin as a piece of paper. It should look like Fig. 1 (actual size). Start rolling the bud from left to right, Fig. 2 and Fig. 3. Roll the right side of the petal back to make it limp, like a real rose petal, Fig. 3. *To make the next petal,* take a small ball of dark pink dough the size of a pea and press, pinch, and flatten it as before. Shape as shown in Fig. 4. Make five petals in this manner. Make the petals nice and thin. (Note: In working with the bread dough, one of the most important steps is to make the dough as flat and paper-thin as possible. This is what gives the bread dough the ceramic-like look.) Shape each petal as shown in Fig. 4, rolling both sides of the petal back to make it look "limp," like a real rose petal. If possible, when creating these bread roses, have a sample rose to work from.

Apply glue on the bottom of each petal as you add the petal to the center. Place the second petal on opposite the opening of the roll on the bud. Add the remaining three petals the same way, using Figs. 5, 6, and 7 as guides. *Be sure petals are same height as the center.* (The most common error when making roses is to add each petal progressively lower, until it looks like a pinecone.) Make nine roses (four for pendant, two for earrings, and three for comb). *To make the leaves,* take a small piece of dough (green, if precolored) and roll it into a ball. Press into a flat piece. Cut to shape using small manicure scissors. With a pin or nail, press lines or veins on the dough leaf. Make about thirteen or fourteen leaves.

Let each rose and leaf dry overnight or until hard. If color was not mixed with the dough, hand paint and shade with the paint of your choice. Glue the roses and leaves to the pendant, earring backs, and comb with tacky glue, using photograph as guide. If desired, trim with dried baby's breath and small bows.

Fig. 1   Fig. 2   Fig. 3   Fig. 4

Fig. 5   Fig. 6   Fig. 7

72

Repairing or Decorating an Old Frame with Bread Dough

Do you have an old antique sculptured picture frame that has been damaged? Using the bread dough recipe (page 71), copy flowers and leaves or other ornaments to fill in the damage, glue into place, paint or gold-leaf the entire frame, and it will look like new. Or you might like to take a plain frame, mold roses, forget-me-nots, and leaves, and build yourself an antique-looking frame as shown in the photograph. If you are adding molded flowers for ornamentation, paint them before gluing.

Bread Dough Necklaces

Give your wardrobe a lift with carrots, bananas, pea pods, and other fruits and vegetables inspired by a trip to the greengrocer, or with whimsical hearts. Bright, gay, colorful jewelry is high fashion and these designs have a lot of charm.

Fruit Necklace

Materials:

Bread dough (see instructions page 71)
1 piece 22-gauge wire
Acrylic paint: red, yellow, orange, light green, and brown
Brush-on glaze
1 barrel clasp (jewelry finding; see page 76)
24″ 20-pound-test fishing line (or more for longer necklace)
About 60 red wooden beads, 5-mm. each (or more for longer necklace)
1 silver tube for crimping line (jewelry finding)
Needle-nosed pliers

Instructions:

Make bread dough as instructed. Shape fruit from bread dough, using drawings as guide for shape and size. Make eight bananas, two apricots, two oranges, two plums, two lemons, and two pears. While still soft, insert wire through sides of fruits to form holes for threading line through. Leave fruits on wire until completely dry. Paint fruit as suggested on drawings. Let dry completely. Brush all surfaces with glaze, making sure to keep hole clear so that line can be threaded through. (To dry-brush the apricot and pear, dip brush into paint and brush on paper towel, eliminating all excess paint and leaving only a slight amount on brush—the brush is

BANANA
paint yellow with brown highlights

APRICOT
paint yellow with orange dry-brushing & brown highlights

ORANGE
paint orange with light green highlights

PLUM
paint brown

LEMON
paint yellow

PEAR
paint light green with yellow dry-brushing & brown highlights

almost "dry" of paint.) *To assemble necklace,* cut rings from end of barrel clasp, Fig. 1. Thread end of line through side A, tie a knot at end, and pull back through side A, so that knot is tight inside barrel, Fig. 2. Cut off excess line. Thread approximately twenty beads onto line (more if longer necklace is desired). Then add fruit, in a balanced pattern, alternating with wooden beads (see photograph). End with twenty more beads (or the same number used at start). Place side B barrel clasp onto line, then slip silver tube on end, pull necklace tight, and "crimp" silver tube tight against the line using needle-nosed pliers, Fig. 3.

Note: There are many kinds of clasps available. You could use clasps and rings from an old necklace instead, if you have them.

Fourteen-Carrot Necklace

(See photo on page 75.)

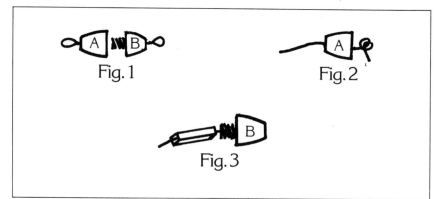

Materials:

Bread dough (see instructions
    page 71)
1 piece 22-gauge wire
Acrylic paint: orange, light
    green, and dark green
Brush-on glaze
1 barrel clasp (jewelry finding,
    see note)
37 green wooden beads ³⁄₈″
    diameter (more for longer
    necklace)
24″ 20-pound-test fishing line
    (more for longer necklace)
1 silver tube for crimping line
    (jewelry finding)
Needle-nosed pliers

Instructions:

Shape fourteen carrots from bread dough, using drawing as guide for shape and size. Insert wire through sides of carrots to form holes to thread line through. Leave carrots on wire until completely dry. Paint carrots orange and tops light green, highlight with dark green on tops and carrot. Let dry completely. Brush entire surface with glaze, making sure to keep hole clear so that line can be threaded through. *To assemble necklace,* attach rings of barrel clasp as described on page 74. Thread twelve wooden beads onto line (more for longer necklace). Thread carrots onto line, alternating with wooden beads as shown in photograph. End with twelve beads (or same number used to start). Attach barrel clasp as described on page 74.

Heart Necklace

(See photo on page 75.)

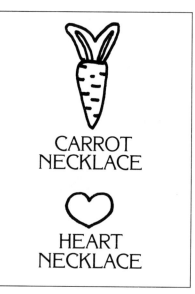

CARROT
NECKLACE

HEART
NECKLACE

Materials:

Bread dough (see instructions
    page 71)
X-acto knife or ³⁄₈″ heart-shaped
    dough press
24 wire eyepins
Red acrylic paint
Brush-on glaze
30″ red satin cording
2 red wooden beads ³⁄₈″ diameter

Instructions:

Roll dough out to ¼ inch thickness and cut ³⁄₈-inch triangle shape. Form triangle into heart shape following drawing. Repeat to make twenty-four hearts. (Hint: We've used a dough press to stamp out heart shapes.) Insert an eyepin in top of each heart. Let dough dry completely. Paint with red acrylic paint. Let dry. Brush glaze onto each heart. Let dry. *To assemble necklace,* find center of cording and tie knot. Thread one heart onto cord. Knot cord ½ inch from first heart. Repeat until you have twelve hearts on one side of cording. Repeat on other side. Add a bead and a knot after last knot at each end (as shown in photo) to complete necklace.

CHAPTER FIVE

"Antique Silver" from Forged Foil

You can give old boxes, containers, or cartons great elegance by covering them with kitchen foil and string, using our forged foil technique.

Forged foil is simply crinkled kitchen aluminum foil or florist's foil pushed, pressed, and shaped to a textured surface to take on the underlying contour and glued in place. Given a final painting and glazing, it looks like expensive antiqued silver.

You may use any kind of foil, providing it does not have a paper or plastic back; it must be pure foil. You may use the technique on any surface: wood, glass, plastic, etc.; on picture frames, on vases, boxes, candlesticks, old lamp bases, bed headboards, trunks, tables, and hundreds of other worn-out or just plain undistinguished objects. You may forge-foil figurines or simply cut designs from cardboard and create wall plaques or pictures. The process is as easy as one, two, three:

1. Glue design of string on the object to be decorated.
2. Crinkle aluminum foil and glue onto design.
3. Antique with black paint, and seal.

Start with the Forged Foil Box (page 78) to learn the technique.

Forged Foil Box

Materials:

An old box with lid
White tacky glue
Aluminum foil
Heavy cord or string, ⅛″
   diameter
Spray or brush-on black acrylic
   paint
Soft cloth
Spray or brush-on glaze for finish

Instructions:

Using a cigar box or other discard, draw a design on the top and sides with pencil, pen, or chalk. Our picture shows a simple daisy. Outline the design with tacky glue. Glue the cord onto the design. Let dry. *To cover,* take a piece of foil a little larger than the section to be covered. Crumple the foil, then straighten it out again, gently. Brush tacky glue over the section to be covered and lay the foil over the design. Press the foil up against the string, starting with the center of the design, until the foil takes on the contour of the string. Be gentle, yet be sure that the foil becomes dimensional and that the design shows up clearly. Cover one section at a time. Cut off the excess foil, leaving just enough to cover the edge of the box and to glue on the inside of the lid to make a nice finished edge. If the foil tears as you press it around the string, simply take a small, torn piece of foil, crinkle it, and glue it in place to cover tear. The small torn piece will blend right in and you will not be able to see your patch. Let dry. When the box is completely covered, let dry overnight before antiquing it.

To antique, spray on or brush on black acrylic paint and *immediately* wipe off paint gently with a soft rag. The black paint will remain in the cracks and crevices and give an antiqued look. Do not use too much paint and if working on a large design, do it section by section so that the paint does not have time to dry before wiping off. It is easier to add more paint than to take off excess. If you want more of the silver to show, do *not* crinkle your foil too much. For more antiquing, crinkle the foil more. This controls the antique look. When the entire box is antiqued, brush on or spray on a coat of glaze to give the box a hard, lasting surface and to give the design a soft sheen.

Forged Foil Plaque

Now that you know the basics of forged foiling, you can create designs of greater intricacy. What is your pleasure . . . an antique car, a gift for a railroad buff, a medieval figure like the horse and chariot in the photograph? You can achieve anything you want.

Items that would ordinarily be made of metal such as ships, cars, and shields make excellent subjects. Floral designs, animals, and people can be very effective, also. The horse and chariot is shown to illustrate the type of detail that is possible with the forged foil technique. Choose your favorite picture, and recreate it with string and foil. Coloring book designs are the simplest ones to recreate, however any designs or patterns from other craft projects or illustrations from magazines or books can serve as patterns for forged foil.

Simply glue string to outline the entire figure, using heavier string for the outline, lighter string for detail. Even candlewicking is excellent, as it shows a lot of texture and gives depth in the finished foiling. Glue on lace, appliqués, gold stars, braids, jewels, etc.—anything with an interesting texture. When foil is pressed into place, it will give form and texture to the outline beneath it.

Materials:

Cardboard for base of design
Velvet or felt remnant for
   background
1 box aluminum foil
White tacky glue
Cord and string of varied
   thickness
Spray or brush-on black acrylic
   paint
Soft cloth
Spray or brush-on glaze for finish
Frame (optional)

Instructions:

Trace pattern onto cardboard. You can foil the entire design, including subject and background, or you can cut out the subject, foil it, and glue it onto a felt or velvet background, as shown. Glue velvet onto cardboard, then paste down the design. Add crinkled foil, a section at a time following instructions for foil box (above). Note in photograph that certain areas such as the chariot wheel and the armor are left a little darker (foil crinkled more). Areas such as horse's body are crinkled less, so that more silver shows through. Antique with black paint as described in the foil box above, and finish with glaze to bring out the luster of the paint. Frame, if desired.

Forged Foil Boudoir Tray

Rickrack and cording were used on a tray from the supermarket. Both top and bottom were foiled, using the techniques described in Forged Foil Box (page 78).

Forged Foil Photo Album

Using the same technique detailed in the preceding foil projects, transfer the pattern shown onto the front of a photo album. Glue cording in place, let dry. Crinkle foil and glue it to the outside, extending foil to inside cover. Antique and seal following instructions for Forged Foil Box (page 78).

1 square equals 4/16 inch

Forged Foil Urn

(See photo on page 79.)

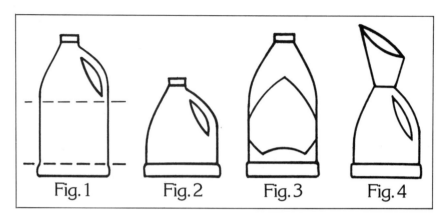

Fig. 1   Fig. 2   Fig. 3   Fig. 4

Materials:

2 half-gallon plastic bleach
   bottles
Wire cutters
White tacky glue
Masking tape 1″ wide
1 box aluminum foil
Cord and string of varied
   thicknesses
Braid or jewels of varied textures
Spray or brush-on black acrylic
   paint
Spray or brush-on glaze for finish

Instructions:

To make the urn, measure up 1½ inches from the bottom of bleach bottle. Draw a line this height around the bottle. Cut the bottle apart on this line, Fig. 1. Most plastic bottles this size have a slight indentation just below the handle. Cut off the top of this line (see dotted line in Fig. 1) and discard center strip. Fit the top down over the bottom section, making the bottle shorter, Fig. 2.

To make the top, trace the pattern, cut out, and lay it onto the second bottle, Fig. 3. Trace around the pattern and cut out the top. Staple the A edge to the B edge. Make the hole in the bottom just large enough to fit the top opening. Glue the urn top onto the bottle section, Fig. 4. Cut a strip of paper 1 inch wide or use a piece of masking tape to fit the area where top and bottom meet. Glue this strip into place. Let dry.

Lay out design. *To add texture,* in addition to the string you can use cut-out cardboard designs, braids, jewels, artificial leaves, pieces of crochet or rope, etc. Glue design down. *After the design is firmly set,* brush glue all over the urn. Take a piece of foil large enough to surround the urn and overlap generously. Crumple the foil lightly, open up again, and

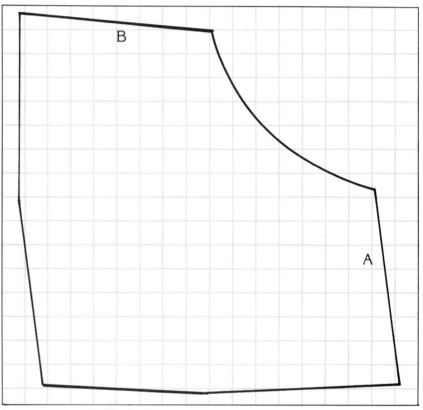

1 square equals ⁴/₁₆ inch

place onto the urn. With fingers, press foil into and around the design. Start to press in the center and work outward. As the foil takes on contour, you may find yourself running out of foil. To add more or to patch, simply tear off a piece of foil from the roll, crumple it, and glue it down. *To antique,* spray or brush on the

paint, *a small section at a time.* Wipe off immediately with a soft cloth until desired black is left in the crevices and the desired silver is showing on the higher areas. Finish by brushing on a coat of glaze to bring out the luster and to create a hard, durable surface that can be cleaned with a damp cloth.

CHAPTER SIX

Fine Designs from Fabric Fragments

Everyone has fabric on hand—leftovers from an earlier project, an old sock, a bit of lace, discarded clothes, and inexpensive remnants too pretty to throw away. From these fragments, you can make hundreds of useful items at a fraction of their cost if store-bought. We've designed sculptured picture frames, soft-sculpture flowers, a jewelry box, and lots more. Even without too much previous craft experience—and even without using a sewing machine—these projects can be easily completed. So enjoy!

Lacy Hearts and Wreaths

Lacy hearts and wreaths look like long-ago crafts, but they are easy to make and treasured today as Christmas ornaments, package-toppers, and the like. So go Victorian and make this sentimental design part of the package when you gift the new baby or the bride.

Lacy Hearts

Materials:

Scrap of cotton lace fabric (old crocheted doily?) about 4″ square
1 white chenille stem
White tacky glue
Pregathered 12″ strip lace trim ⅝″ wide for edge
18″ ⅛″ wide ribbon
Dried baby's breath for trim
3 ribbon floribunda roses (see instructions page 160)
6″ gold cord for hanger (optional)

Instructions:

Glue lace fabric to chenille stem bent into heart shape. (Hint: Lay chenille stem on a plastic bag when gluing and when glue dries, you can just pull it off.) When dry, cut excess fabric away from the outside of the heart shape, leaving approximately ¾ inch all around; glue this excess ¾ inch around chenille stem to back of heart. Let dry. Glue lace trim to front edges of heart. For looped bow, fold ribbon back and forth at 3-inch intervals and secure loops at center with a piece of thread. Trim with ribbon roses and dried baby's breath. Glue a hanger to top of heart, if desired.

Lacy Wreaths

Materials:

½ yd. seam binding
½ yd. lace trim
Saw (jigsaw or hacksaw)
1 wooden macrame ring or curtain ring ¾″ diameter
White tacky glue
Narrow ribbon, dried flowers, or silk flowers for trim
6″ gold cord for hanger (optional)

Instructions:

To form casing for ring, pin seam binding to wrong side of lace. Sew down both sides of binding 1/16 inch from edge. If ring is not already split, use a saw and cut through one side. Spread ring apart at cut and feed ring through casing, continuing to slide lace all the way around ring to form gathers. Tack ends of lace together, forming a continuous circle of fabric. Trim wreath with bows, dried flowers, or silk flowers. Glue hanger to top of wreath, if desired.

Fashion Lady on a Spoon

Make several of these as door prizes, wall hangings, or to be raffled off the day of the club fashion-show fundraising event. They need not be identical, so use whatever scraps of felt, fabric, and lace you—and the ladies of the committee who are helping—have available.

Materials:

Yellow braid, burlap, or yarn for hair
Wooden or plastic spoon about 13″ high for face and body
2 moving eyes 10 mm.
Red heart-shaped sequin or felt cutout for mouth
9″ x 12″ felt for hat and cape
2 chenille stems for arms
2 plastic hands (from craft supply store)
Fabric scraps for skirt
Compass for drawing skirt circles
1⅓ yds. lace trim ⅝″ wide
White tacky glue
Needle and thread
Gold cord for hanger (optional)

Instructions:

Glue "hair" along the top back-side of spoon, and cut to shape. Glue eyes and mouth in place. Cut *bonnet* from felt, using pattern as guide; glue it on along outside edge of spoon as shown in photograph. Twist chenille stems together for *arms*. Dip ends in glue and slip ends into hands. Let dry. Glue arms onto spoon handle approximately 5 inches from bottom. Cut circle 18 inches in diameter from fabric for *dress*. Cut circle 2 inches in diameter from the middle. Using needle and thread, run a basting stitch around the 2-inch circle. Gather to fit spoon handle. Glue in place underneath arms. Glue or sew lace trim around outside edge of fabric at waistline. Cut *cape* from felt, using pattern as guide. With needle and thread, run a basting stitch along straight edge of cape. Gather to fit around spoon handle. Glue in place over arms. Tie remaining lace trim in bow around neckline. If you wish, glue hanger to back of head.

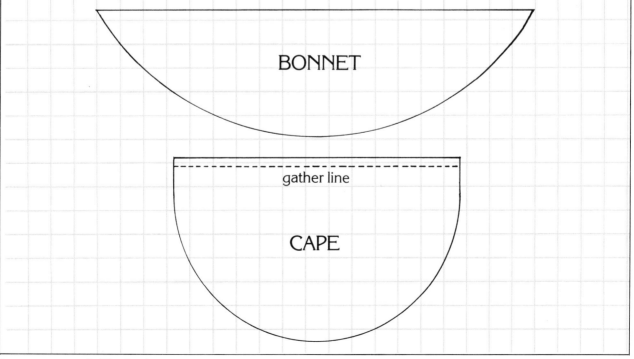

BONNET

gather line

CAPE

1 square equals ⁷/₁₆ inch

Padded Double Picture Frame

Materials:

4 pieces cardboard (not
   corrugated), 5½" x 7" each
4 fabric scraps, 5½" x 7" each
White tacky glue
Polyester batting 1" thick
Straight pins
24" lace or eyelet trim

Instructions:

To make back of frame: Lay two pieces of cardboard side by side on the table ¼ inch apart. Cut a strip of fabric 1½ inches x 7 inches. Glue fabric to the two cardboard pieces, maintaining the ¼-inch space between to form a "hinge." Cut two pieces of fabric 12 inches x 15 inches. Lay one piece on the table, wrong side up. Center back of frame on fabric. Apply a line of glue ¼ inch from edge around all four edges of cardboard. Pull fabric around edges and over cardboard and press down onto glue. Smooth down. Turn neat square corners. Spread glue evenly over remaining cardboard side, lay other piece of fabric over, and smooth down. Trim off excess.

To make front of frame: Cut oval from center of cardboard on two pieces, following pattern. Each frame front is made separately. Cut a piece of batting 5½ inches x 7 inches. Cut a piece of fabric 6½ inches x 8 inches. Lay fabric wrong side up on table. Center batting on fabric. Lay frame front (with oval cut out) on batting. Apply a line of glue ¼ inch from edge around all four edges of cardboard. Pull fabric around edges and over cardboard and press down onto glue. Smooth down. Turn neat square corners. Cut batting from oval, being careful not to cut fabric underneath. Cut a small opening in fabric in center of oval, then cut clips out to edge of batting approximately ½ inch apart. Apply line of glue on cardboard ½ inch from edge of oval cutout. Bring slit pieces up

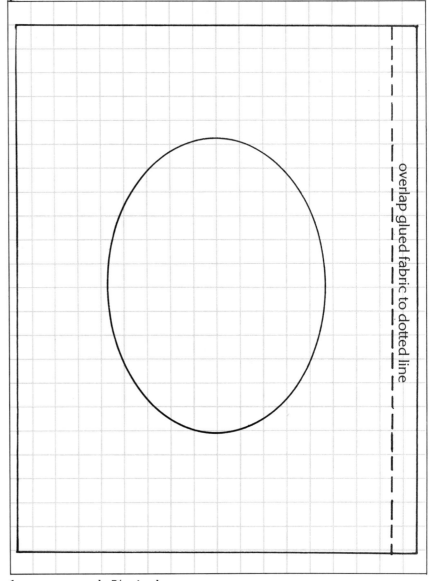

1 square equals ⁵⁄₁₆ inch

overlap glued fabric to dotted line

through oval and press down over glue. Put a straight pin through each piece into cardboard to hold until dry. If you want trim around edge of frame, apply a line of glue on wrong side of frame front ¼ inch from edge and glue trim in place. Repeat process to make second frame front.

To assemble double frame: Glue two front frame pieces to back piece, lining up outside and top edges. Apply glue around side and bottom edges, leaving top edge unglued so pictures can be slipped in.

Padded Single Picture Frame

A single picture frame can be made the same way, cutting the amount of fabric in half and making only one front and back.

Padded Holiday Picture Frames

Bell Picture Frame

Materials:

Illustration board or cardboard
(not corrugated)
Polyester batting ½" thick
3 fabric scraps, each 7" square
White tacky glue
Straight pins
18" piping or lace trim (optional)
Ribbon, small wooden bead or
round bell for trim (optional)
6" narrow ribbon for hanger

Instructions:

Cut two bell shapes from cardboard, using pattern as guide. Cut center oval shape from middle of one bell shape. Cut one bell shape from batting, using pattern as guide. Cut three pieces of fabric approximately 1 inch larger than bell all the way around.

To make front of bell: Place one piece of fabric on table wrong side up. Center bell-shaped batting piece on top of fabric. Place the cardboard bell with the center cut out on top of batting. Apply line of glue all around edge of cardboard, approximately ½ inch from edge. Gently pull fabric up and press over glue. Continue around entire bell. To help fabric lie flat, you may have to make a small cut where bell curves at each side. Clip piece of batting from oval

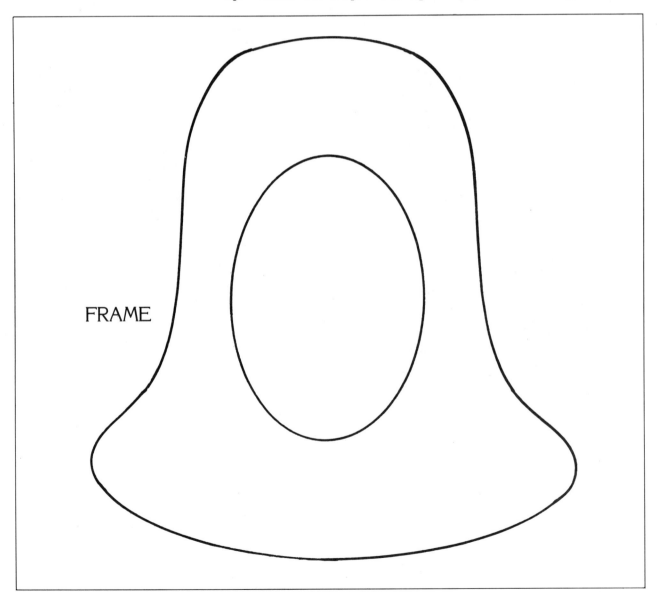

FRAME

Cornhusk Tree
(Project on page 12)

Petal Painting
(Project on page 16)

Three-Tiered Trinket Box and Jewelry Cases
(Projects on pages 101 and 102)

Matchstick Picture
Frame, Desk Organizer,
and Pencil Cup
(Projects on pages
50 and 51)

Homemade Paper and Botanical Print
(Project on page 19)

Soft-Sculpture Flowers
(Projects on pages 94 and 97)

Antiqued Plant Containers
(Projects on page 28)

Tissue Painting
(Project on page 38)

Spool Horse, Train, and Girl
(Projects on pages 46—49)

Children's Party Clown
(Project on page 152)

Cards and Ornaments
(Projects on pages 136 and 138)

Bread Dough Jewelry
(Projects on page 71)

Bread Dough Jewelry
(Projects on page 74)

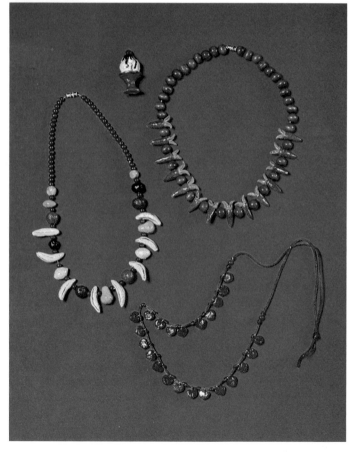

Corn Flake Tree
(Project on page 70)

Fabric Frames
(Projects on pages 86–90)

Muffin Cup Wreath
(Project on page 25)

Paper Plate Decor
(Projects on pages 26 and 27)

Forged Foil Boudoir Tray
and Photo Album
(Projects on page 80)

cutout area, being careful not to clip fabric underneath. Clip a small hole in fabric in center of oval cutout. Starting from center, clip to edge of oval cutout and batting, being careful not to clip batting. Continue clipping fabric from center at ½-inch intervals around edge. Apply line of glue around edge of oval cutout. Pull each clipped piece of fabric over edge and glue onto cardboard surface. Push straight pins through each piece of fabric into cardboard to help hold until glue dries.

To make back of bell: Place second piece of fabric on table wrong side up. Center cardboard bell on top of fabric. Apply line of glue around edge of cardboard approx-

imately ½ inch from edge. Gently pull fabric up and over glue. Continue around entire bell. To help fabric lie flat, you may have to make a small clip where bell curves at each side. Apply glue to entire cardboard surface and glue on square piece of fabric. Press down smoothly and trim off excess fabric around edge. Let both front and back dry completely.

To assemble: Apply a line of glue around sides and bottom of wrong side of front of bell. Glue front to back, leaving top open to slide picture in. If trim is desired, glue a piece of piping or lace trim around edge of bell. A wooden bead or round bell can be glued along bottom edge for clapper.

Trim top of bell with a bow and glue a loop of ribbon to back for a hanger.

Bootie Picture Frame

(See photo on page 89.)

Follow directions for Bell Picture Frame. Glue lace trim around edges of cardboard between layers before attaching frame front and back. If lace trim is desired along top of bootie, glue to wrong side of front piece. Then glue front to back along sides and bottom, leaving top open for picture to slide in.

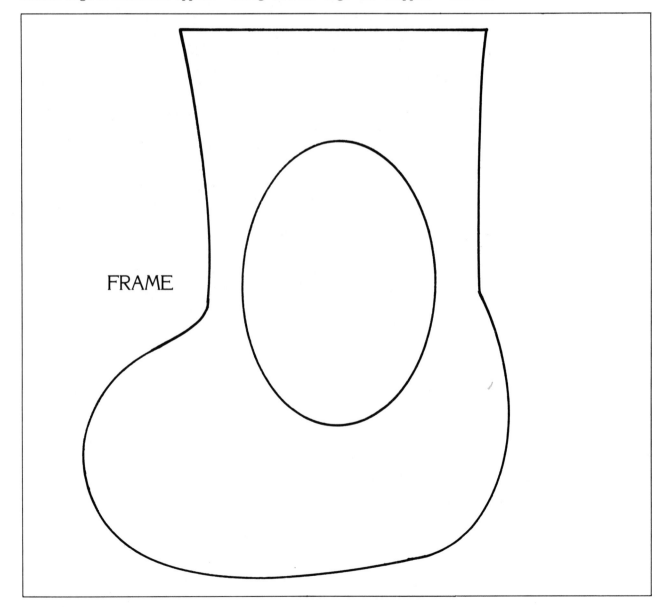

FRAME

Sock Bunny

(See photo on page 93.)

Materials:

1 white girl's sock
Polyester fiberfill for stuffing
White thread and sewing needle
2 small black beads for eyes
Pink embroidery thread and
    embroidery needle for nose
Small fabric flowers for trim
White tacky glue
12" x 12" fabric scrap for blanket
    (cut with pinking shears to
    prevent fraying)
12" narrow ribbon for trim

Instructions:

To make ears, turn sock inside out and stitch securely down middle from toe 1½ inches, over ⅛ inch, and back up to toe, as shown in drawing. Cut sock between stitching. Turn right side out and stuff ears and head—approximately 3½ inches down from top of ears. *To create neckline,* stitch with running stitch (simple stitches of even length), using double thread for extra strength, approximately 3½ inches from top of ears. Gather, wrap excess thread twice around neck and pull taut, knot and tie thread off at back of head. Exposed threads will be covered by blanket and tie. Stuff sock for a length of 5 inches to make *body;* cut off excess sock. Turn ends in and stitch together with small, invisible stitches, closing bottom. Stitch beads in place for *eyes,* doubling thread for strength and bringing needle through back of neck, out eye placement area, through bead, into sock and out other eye placement area, through bead, and back in through sock to back of neck. Repeat several times. This procedure indents the eye areas, giving contours to the face. Tie thread securely at back of neck. *For nose,* using drawing as guide, work satin stitch with pink embroidery thread. Thread may be

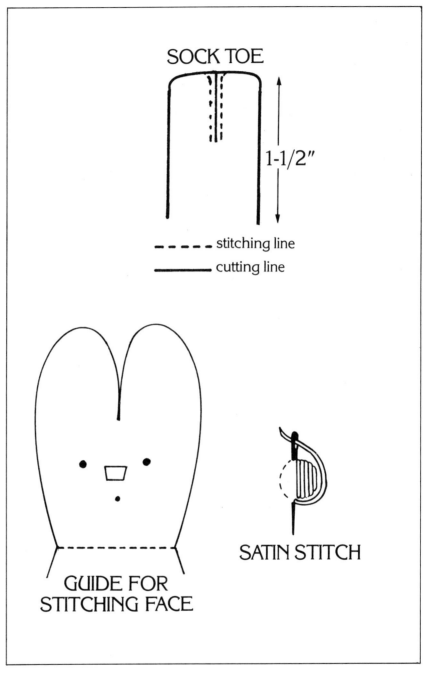

SOCK TOE

1-1/2"

- - - - - stitching line
——— cutting line

GUIDE FOR STITCHING FACE

SATIN STITCH

tied off in nose area, under the stitching, or pulled through to back of neck and tied off. *For mouth,* use double white thread and come through back of neck, out side of mouth area, in other side of mouth, and out back of neck again. Pull taut to give con-

tour to mouth (see photo). Tie thread securely at back of neck. Glue flowers between ears for trim. Place bunny in blanket and wrap. Stitch loose blanket ends together at bottom of bunny if desired. Tie ribbon around outside of blanket at bunny's neckline.

Sock Chicken

Materials:

1 yellow infant sock
Polyester fiberfill for stuffing
Sewing needle and thread
Embroidery needle and thread
Fabric scraps for beak and wings
White tacky glue
2 small black plastic eyes
8″ narrow ribbon for necktie
Miniature straw hat or felt
  scraps for hat (optional)

Instructions:

Fill toe of sock with stuffing. Create *neckline* approximately 1½ inches from toe with running stitches. Gather, knot, and tie off thread. Stitches will be covered later by ribbon. Continue to stuff *body* to 3 inches in length. Fold ends in and stitch together with small invisible stitches, forming tail. Using contrasting or matching thread, stitch three running embroidery stitches (simple stitches of even length), at end of tail, to form feathers, as shown in drawing. Cut *wings* from fabric, using pattern as guide. Glue or stitch wrong sides together, folding in raw edges. Glue or stitch wings in place on sides of chicken. Glue *eyes* in place. Glue four thicknesses of fabric together. Cut *beak* from fabric, using pattern as guide. Fold where indicated and glue or stitch beak to sock, using photo as placement guide. Tie ribbon around neck. Glue straw hat to head, if desired (or make hat from felt scraps).

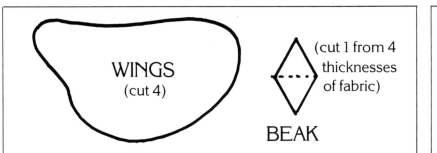

WINGS (cut 4)

BEAK (cut 1 from 4 thicknesses of fabric)

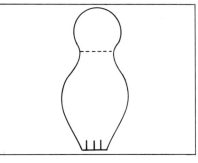

Sock Snowman

Materials:

1 white infant sock for body
Polyester fiberfill for stuffing
2 black plastic eyes
White tacky glue
Small piece hot pink felt for
  cheeks
1 red infant sock for cap
Needle and thread: white; black
  for mouth
8″ ribbon for trim

Instructions:

For snowman's head, fill toe of white sock with stuffing, forming a ball 2 inches in diameter. Create *neckline* approximately 2 inches from toe with running stitches. Knot and tie off thread. Stitches will be covered later by ribbon necktie. Continue to fill *body* with stuffing, making a ball 2½ inches in diameter. Cut off excess sock. Fold ends in and stitch together with small, invisible stitches. Glue eyes in place. *To make nose,* with running stitch, stitch a circle ¼ inch in diameter. Slightly tighten stitch to "pucker" nose. Stitch *mouth* with black thread in running stitch as shown in photograph. Tie off thread in cheek area where exposed thread ends will be covered by cheek hearts. Cut two hearts from pink felt. Glue hearts in place for cheeks. *To make cap,* cut off 2 inches of red sock cuff. On wrong side, gather cut edge with a basting stitch and pull together. Knot and tie off end. Turn cap right side out and place on snowman's head. Turn finished edge of cap up, forming brim. Tie ribbon around neck.

Soft-Sculpture Flowers with Stamens

Materials (for one flower, 10″ from tip to tip):

Print or plain fabric scraps for petals and leaves
Compass
Needle and thread
Polyester batting 1″ thick
Brown felt scraps for stamens and calyx
White tacky glue
3 pieces 26-gauge bare wire, 12″ each
3 pieces 18-gauge covered wire, 18″ each
Brown ½″ florist's tape

Instructions:

Cut ten petals from fabric, using pattern as guide. With right sides together and a ½ inch seam allowance, stitch five petals together, side A to B, forming circle. Repeat process with remaining five petals. Cut a circle 10 inches in diameter from batting. Place stitched petal pieces right sides together with batting on top. Sew around outside of petals along sewing line. Trim and clip edges. Cut out center of batting. Turn right side out. Hand or machine baste around inside circle. *To make stamens,* cut four stamen pieces from felt, using pattern as guide. Cut one piece 18-gauge wire in half. Glue two stamens together with an 18-gauge wire between as shown on pattern. Make two stamens. Insert stamens through center hole of petals. Gather basting stitches to tighten petals around stamen wire. Using a 26-gauge wire, wrap bottom of petals tightly to secure to stamen wire. Tape stem with brown tape, covering exposed wires. Cut *calyx* from brown felt, using pattern as guide. Cut small hole in center of calyx as shown. Using pattern as guide, snip out from hole (to allow

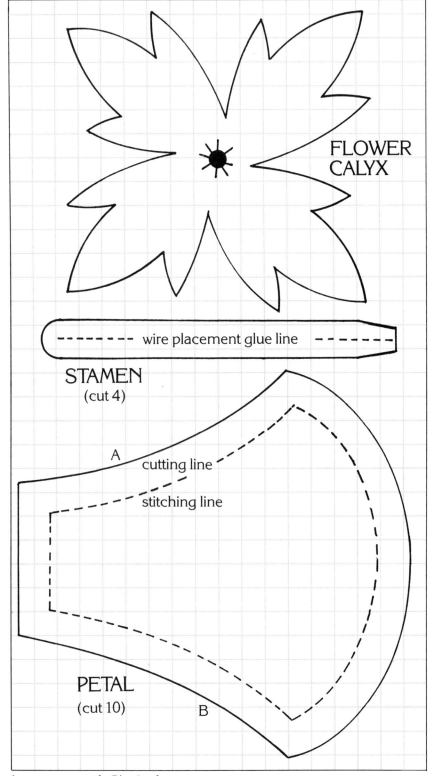

FLOWER CALYX

wire placement glue line

STAMEN (cut 4)

A   cutting line

stitching line

PETAL (cut 10)

B

1 square equals 5/16 inch

94

calyx to fit over taped stem). Glue calyx to back of flower.

To make leaves, cut four leaf shapes from fabric, using pattern as guide. Place fabric right sides together and stitch along sewing line. Leave bottom open for turning. Turn right side out and stitch along stitching guide line to form casing for wire. Insert 18-gauge wire into casing all around leaf, leaving excess at one end for stem. Wire bottom of leaf to stem with 26-gauge wire. Tape stem with brown tape, covering exposed wires. Make two leaves. Tape leaves onto flower stem, the first leaf approximately 6 inches from bottom of flower and the second leaf approximately 4 inches from the first.

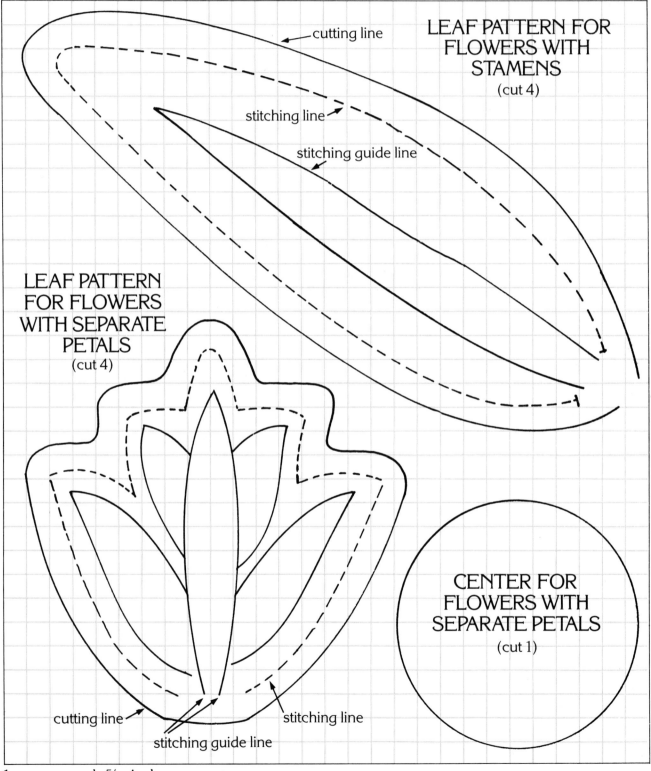

LEAF PATTERN FOR FLOWERS WITH STAMENS
(cut 4)

cutting line

stitching line

stitching guide line

LEAF PATTERN FOR FLOWERS WITH SEPARATE PETALS
(cut 4)

CENTER FOR FLOWERS WITH SEPARATE PETALS
(cut 1)

cutting line

stitching guide line

stitching line

1 square equals ⁵/₁₆ inch

Soft-Sculpture Flowers with Separate Petals

(See photo on page 95.)

We've shown this and the preceding flower made with contrasting petals, leaves, and centers, but you might want to match your one-color living room scheme with a one-color flower arrangement—with variety achieved through texture only. Use fabric remnants like velvet for petals, shiny satin for leaves, and rough linen or burlap for center.

Materials: (for one flower, 12″ from tip to tip):

Plain fabric scraps for petals, center, and leaves
Polyester batting ½″ thick
Needle and thread
8 pieces 18-gauge covered wire, 18″ each
Fiberfill scraps for flower center
4 pieces 26-gauge bare wire, 12″ each
Brown ½″ florist's tape
Brown felt scrap for calyx
White tacky glue

Instructions:

Cut ten petals, using pattern as guide. Cut five petal shapes from batting. Place two petals right sides together, with a piece of batting on top. Stitch along sewing line, with a ½-inch seam allowance, leaving bottom open for turning. Turn right side out and stitch along two stitching guide lines to form casing for wire. Repeat process to make a total of five petals. Fold 18-gauge wire ½ inch from end to form hook, and insert into casing. Gather fabric onto wire until wire comes out at other end. Twist wire at bottom of petal to hold. Repeat process on remaining petals.

Cut out *center of flower* from fabric, using pattern on page 96

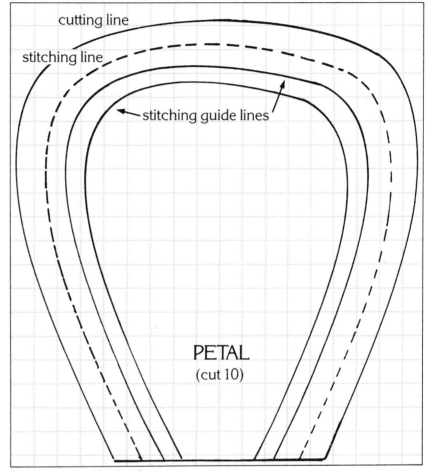

1 square equals 5/16 inch

as guide. Baste around edge of fabric center. Fill center with fiberfill or batting and gather basting stitches to form a ball. Grasp fabric at bottom of center and wrap tightly with a 26-gauge wire. Gather five petals together, overlapping evenly, with flower center in middle. Tape all six wires together with brown florist's tape. Tape all the way down to bottom of stems. Cut *calyx* from brown felt, using calyx pattern for Soft-Sculpture Flowers with Stamens (page 94) as guide. Cut small hole in center of calyx as shown. Using pattern as guide, snip out from hole (to allow calyx

to fit over taped stem). Glue calyx to back of flower.

Cut four *leaves* from fabric, using pattern on page 96 as guide. Cut two leaf shapes from batting. Place two leaves right side together, with a piece of batting on top, and stitch along sewing line. Leave bottom open for turning. Turn right side out and stitch along stitching guide lines. Repeat process to make second leaf. Insert 18-gauge wire in middle casing on leaf. Tape bottom of leaf to wire with brown florist's tape. Attach leaves to flower stem by taping one 6 inches and the other 10 inches from flower.

Clipboard with Cat

This decorated clipboard is one of those practical items that just make people purr with pleasure at flea-market stands and bazaars.

Materials:

Fabric scraps
Polyester batting 1″ thick for head, ½″ thick for paws
Needle and thread to match fabric
Embroidery needle and black embroidery thread
2 moving eyes 20 mm.
White tacky glue
Waxed dental floss
Clipboard

Instructions:

Cut two heads and four paws from fabric, using pattern as guide. Cut one piece 1 inch batting to same size as head; two pieces ½ inch batting to match paws. *To make paw,* place fabric right sides together with batting on top. Sew paw using ½ inch seam allowance. Leave opening at bottom for turning. Trim seam, clip at curves, and then turn paw right side out. Close opening with small, invisible stitches. Repeat process to make second paw. Using black embroidery thread, sew paw detail with straight stitches, using pattern as guide. *To make cat's head,* place fabric right sides together with batting on top. Sew head using ½ inch seam allowance. Leave opening at bottom for turning. Trim seam, clip at curves, and then turn head right side out. Close opening with small, invisible stitches. Using a basting stitch at base of ears, gather slightly and tie thread off. Glue eyes in place. Using black embroidery thread, run a loose stitch across nose, using pattern as guide for placement. Place finger under stitch to keep it loose.

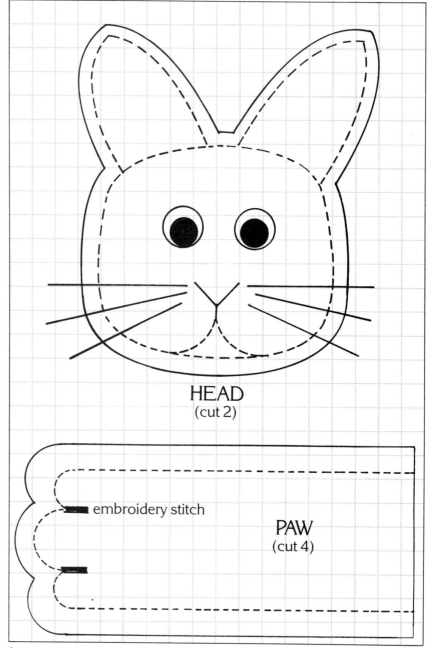

HEAD
(cut 2)

embroidery stitch

PAW
(cut 4)

1 square equals ⁶/₁₆ inch

Bring thread out the back of cat's head and bring under chin and loop it under and then over nose stitch. Loop it back down chin and remove finger and pull thread to form a Y shape. Bring thread to back of the cat's head and tie off securely. *To make whiskers,* cut dental floss into six 2-inch lengths and glue to face, using pattern as guide. Glue head to clip on clipboard and glue paws to wood by bringing excess fabric on paw around to back.

Puffed Wreath

Make it from burlap,
gingham, felt, or a
host of other materials.
It is quick and easy,
inexpensive
and durable.

Materials:

Fabric scraps
Polyester fiberfill
Needle and thread
Beveled plastic foam wreath 24″
    diameter
White tacky glue or hot glue
Pregathered eyelet or lace trim
    for outside of wreath

Instructions:

Cut 125 circles from fabric scraps: 75 circles 4″ diameter, 25 circles 3″ diameter, and 25 circles 2″ diameter. Sew outside edge of each circle with a basting stitch ¼ inch from edge. Place generous ball of fiberfill in middle of each circle and pull basting stitches to gather fabric around ball. Knot end of thread to hold fabric puff securely. Glue large puffs to plastic foam wreath, filling in with smaller puffs (see photograph). Glue lace trim to outside back edge of wreath for trim.

Padded Three-Tiered Trinket Box

You'll have to save three kitchen match-box containers for this one, but it's worth doing. Make it in a provincial fabric to match the bedspread in a girl's room. With some adaptation of the procedure suggested here, you could cover the box in wallpaper remnants, rather than fabric.

Materials:

3 match boxes (with slide-out
   drawers)
Fabric scraps
Polyester batting ¼" thick
White tacky glue
3 wooden beads 10 mm.
3 small pieces 26-gauge wire
Straight pins

Instructions:

Separate drawers from frames of boxes and set aside. Glue three frames together, one on top of the other. Let dry. Cut fabric to cover outside of box, measuring two pieces 5¾ inches x 5½ inches and two pieces 6 inches x 4 inches. Cut two pieces of batting for sides, measuring 4¾ inches x 4½ inches. Glue batting to sides of box. (Batting can also be used on top of box, if desired.) Glue 6-inch x 4-inch fabric pieces to top and bottom of box, folding and gluing excess fabric to inside front and back. Extend excess fabric on sides over batting and glue in place. Fold top edge of remaining two pieces of fabric under ½ inch to form finished edge. Glue along top side edges of box. Fold excess fabric to inside of box, clipping fabric where boxes are glued together. Fold bottom edge of fabric under to form finished edge along bottom, again gluing in place to hold. Use straight pins where needed to help hold fabric while

glue is drying. Cut three pieces of fabric 2½ inches x 3½ inches for drawer fronts. Glue fabric to fronts of drawers, folding and gluing excess to sides and bottom and inside drawers. *For drawer pulls,* insert wire through middle of bead and twist wire to secure. Cut wire off 1 inch from bead. Poke wire through middle center front of drawer and fold wire over to hold. Cover exposed wire by gluing scrap of fabric approximately 1 inch square over it. Let dry and reinsert drawers into box.

Jewelry Cases from Candy Boxes

At the price of chocolates today, even the box they are packaged in is a treasure, and we've made it even more so by converting it into a case for your gems. A ribbon-rose bouquet on top makes it even sweeter.

Materials:

Candy box (heart- or egg-shaped)
Fabric scrap large enough to cover and overlap box lid
White tacky glue
Polyester batting ½" thick
Optional trimmings: lace, ribbon, ribbon floribunda roses (see instructions page 160)
Fabric scraps for lining (optional)

Instructions:

Cut one piece of fabric large enough to cover top and sides of candy-box lid and to overlap inside edge ½ inch. Cut batting to size of top of lid and glue it on. Coat sides and inside ¼ inch of lid with glue. Place fabric over batting and press down on glued sides, smoothing edges. Clip excess fabric to edge of lid at ½-inch intervals and fold to inside glue line. Smooth edges. Glue lace trim to outside edge of lid, and trim top with ribbon roses and/or other trimmings, if desired. Inside of box can be lined with fabric scraps.

CHAPTER SEVEN

Container Creativity

Each day, most of us throw away at least half a dozen containers, jar lids, bottles, and other debris attesting to our meal-preparation customs. Even if your career keeps you too busy for real cooking, you're sure to have such garbage-pail fillers as a maraschino-cherries jar, a little tub left from the carried-in order of soup, or a pie tin that the spinach quiche from the neighborhood gourmet shop was baked in. There's no doubt that the residue of modern lifestyles is omnipresent. And equally true: There's no doubt that we would be helping the ecology tremendously if we found ways to use this debris, or at least some of it. That's what we have done in this chapter: presented you with many deliciously appealing designs that will not only help save the ecology—for some people too abstract an idea to be truly meaningful—but also save money—and *that's* a concept that interests all of us.

Bottle Angel

Materials:

4½" tall bottle (we used a maraschino cherry bottle) for body

Gold spray paint, or gold acrylic paint

2½" diameter plastic foam ball for head

X-acto knife

White tacky glue

Acrylic paint: flesh-color, red, pink

Curly angel hair (available at craft stores)

Narrow gold cord for hair ties

1 white chenille stem for halo

2 yds. gold braid (we've used self-adhesive)

Black construction paper for eyelashes

Gold foil or gold paper for wings, collar, hands

Instructions:

For body, spray or paint bottle gold. Set aside to dry. To achieve contour on face, slightly roll an indentation into plastic foam ball on table edge, as shown in Fig. 1. *To make mouth,* scoop out approximately ½ inch deep with an X-acto knife, following Fig. 1 for shape. Do not discard cutout, as it will be used for nose. *To form nose,* press foam cutout together, using Fig. 1 as guide for size. Glue and pin in place on head. Paint mouth red. Paint cheek area pink. Glue angel hair on top of head, leaving some hair trailing down side of head for pigtails. Tie two small bows from gold cord. Glue and pin in place on sides of head for pigtail effect. Shape chenille stem into *halo,* following Fig. 2. Cover halo with gold braid, using photo as guide. Push end of chenille stem into center back of head and bend stem up to bring halo in line over head. Cut two *eyelashes* from black construction paper, following pattern. Glue eyelashes in place, using Fig. 1 as guide. Cut wings, hands, collar, and arms from gold foil or gold paper, following patterns on page 105. Trim with gold braid as shown in photograph.

Glue head to bottom of bottle. Glue collar around head, forming neck. Glue arms in place, using photo as guide. Glue wings in place on back of bottle. Trim cap of bottle with gold braid, forming skirt bottom.

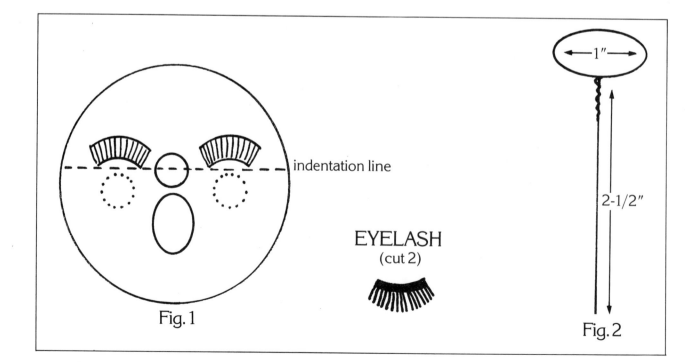

indentation line

Fig. 1

EYELASH
(cut 2)

1"

2-1/2"

Fig. 2

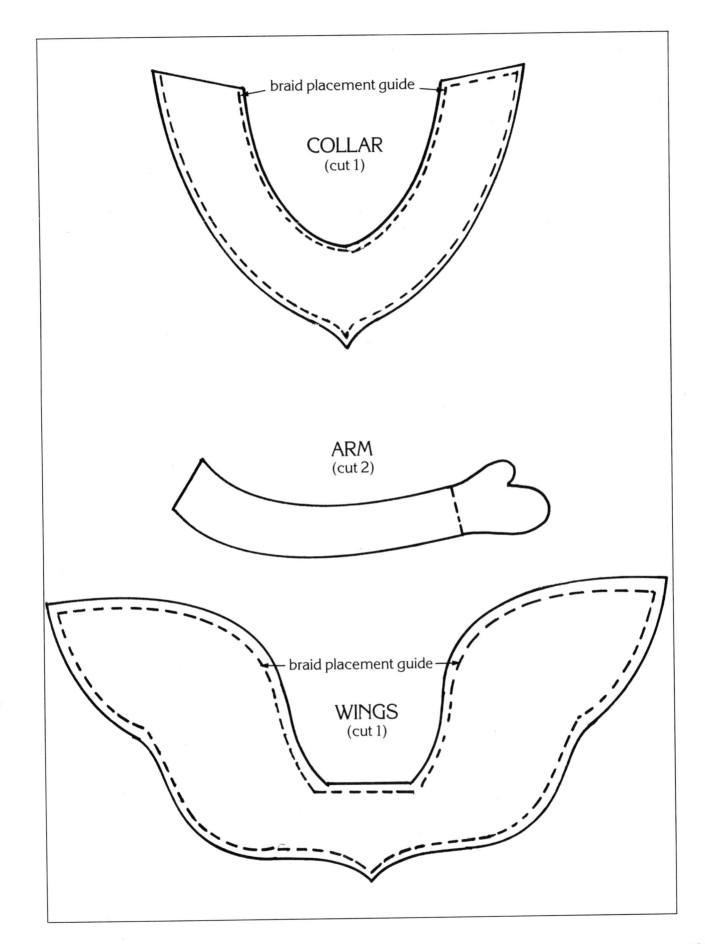

braid placement guide

COLLAR
(cut 1)

ARM
(cut 2)

braid placement guide

WINGS
(cut 1)

Egg Carton Jewel Case

Keep your jewelry organized in the individual compartments of the egg carton . . . and put some pizzazz on the case, too.

Materials:

1 pressed paper egg carton
Assorted trims, appliqués, laces
White tacky glue
Acrylic paints (we've used ivory and light blue for the carton; pink, yellow, and green for the trim)
Brown antiquing spray
Soft cloth
Spray or brush-on varnish

Instructions:

Glue trim to outside of egg carton lid as desired. Paint inside and outside of carton as desired. Paint the trim in contrasting colors. Let paint dry. Antique carton by spraying a small section at a time with antiquing spray and wiping immediately with a soft cloth. Antique all of outside surface. Let dry. Seal surface with a spray or brush-on varnish sealer.

Card Holder

This clever organizer will hold loads of cards, so make one up for your household Christmas, and store another one in case you need a gift for a convalescent, since there's never enough space on a hospital bedside table for all the cards that arrive. Each loop of yarn can hold another card, all around the can.

Materials:

1 coffee can or large juice can
1 skein yarn
Cardboard or illustration board
Felt to match yarn
White tacky glue
Gold braid or rickrack
Optional trimmings: silk flowers, pinecone and berry cluster (see instructions page 158), ribbon, Christmas ornaments, etc.

Instructions:

Remove top and bottom from can. Wrap yarn around and around can lengthwise in a single layer, as shown in photograph, until entire surface is covered. Tie off end and glue to secure. Cut cardboard slightly larger than inside measurement of can top and bottom. Cut two pieces of felt the same size as the cardboard. Glue felt to one side of each cardboard piece. Place felt-covered cardboards onto can and glue in place. Glue braid or rickrack around top rim. Add other trimmings to top, if desired.

Milk Carton Picnic Basket

A loaf of bread, a jug of wine, and a handmade basket to carry them in . . . that's chic! Add plates and stuff and now all signals are "go" for alfresco.

Materials:

3 half-gallon waxed cardboard
    milk cartons
White tacky glue
Heavy-duty stapler
1 cardboard box, 4" x 11½" x 6"
    deep
Cardboard or illustration board
1 yd. sturdy small-print fabric
Eyelet trim and rickrack
    (optional)

Instructions:

Cut milk cartons to height of 6 inches. Discard tops. Glue and staple the cartons side by side, Fig. 1. Glue cartons onto cardboard box, Fig. 2, again stapling for added support. Cut a strip of cardboard 2 inches wide and 24½ inches long to glue along outside of side and bottom seams for more strength. Clip excess at ends of strip to fit to inside of basket and glue in place. Cut fabric to fit inside compartments, gluing bottom pieces in first, then side pieces. Fold side pieces over top edges to cover and glue to outside. Cut fabric for bottom of basket, adding 1 inch all around. Glue to bottom, gluing excess to sides. Cut fabric for sides and ends, adding 1 inch all around. Glue fabric end pieces in place, gluing excess to sides of basket. Fold under raw exposed edges at top and bottom and glue in place. Glue fabric side pieces in place, folding under raw edges and gluing in place. Let dry. *To make handles,* cut two fabric strips 2½ inches x 36 inches. Overlap and glue edges to form a 1½-inch strip, Fig. 3. Glue straps in place, starting at bottom of basket. Brush glue onto wrong side of strap. Bring strap up onto side of basket, letting it extend up for handle. Curve it around and bring it down on the same side, gluing other end of same strip to same side and to bottom, Fig. 4. Repeat on other side. Glue trim to outside of basket, if desired.

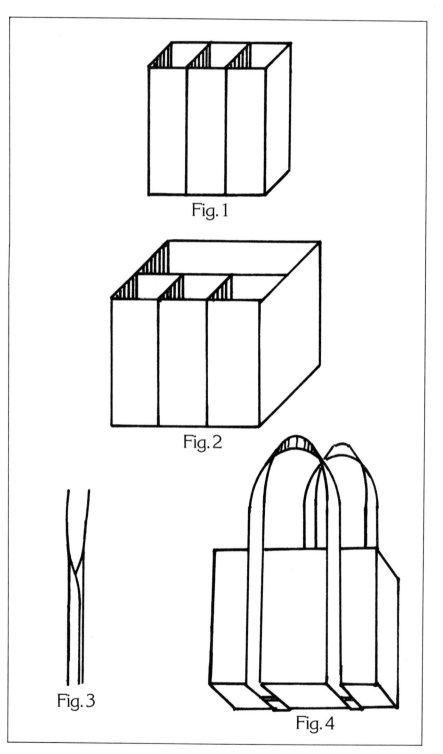

Fig. 1

Fig. 2

Fig. 3

Fig. 4

Strainer Reindeer

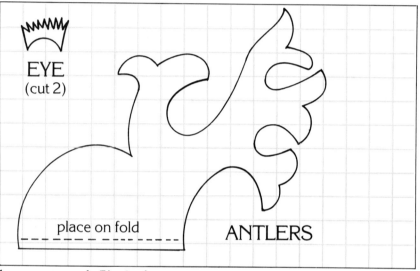

Materials:

1 piece
  lightweight
  cardboard
Felt scraps:
  light brown,
  black,
  and red
White tacky glue
1 small strainer
1 red ¾" pom-pom
1 small pinecone and berry
  cluster (see instructions page
  158), dried baby's breath, and
  narrow ribbon for trim
1"-wide ribbon for bow

Instructions:

Cut *antlers* from cardboard, following pattern. Glue light brown felt to each side of antlers. Cut felt to shape of antlers. Glue antlers to frame of strainer as shown in photograph. Cut two *eyes* from black felt, using pattern as guide, and glue in place as shown in photograph. For *nose,* glue on pompom as shown in photograph. Cut *mouth* from ½-inch length of rickrack, or cut mouth shape from red felt, and glue in place. Glue pinecone cluster or other trims between antlers. Tie bows around handle just below "chin" as a final touch.

EYE
(cut 2)

place on fold

ANTLERS

1 square equals ⁷⁄₁₆ inch

Margarine-Container Mushroom Bank

(See photo on page 113.)

Materials:

1 small round margarine
  container for cap
1 paper cup approx. 4" high x
  2½" wide, for stem
Acrylic paint to match fabric
Fabric scraps
White tacky glue
Compass for drawing cap circle
Felt for free-form shapes on
  mushroom cap

Instructions:

Set bottom of cup on top of margarine lid and mark line around cup onto lid. Remove cup and cut circle from margarine lid. Paint rim of margarine lid. Let dry. *To make stem,* cover outside of cup by gluing fabric down, extending excess fabric to inside lip of cup and gluing down. Cover top of margarine lid with fabric, gluing in place. Trim fabric to fit. Set cup upside down on table and slip margarine lid over bottom of cup, until approximately ¼ inch of cup extends through hole. Glue in place.

To make mushroom cap, cut circle 10 inches in diameter from fabric. Glue to outside of margarine container, clipping fabric where needed to help fabric lie flat. Smooth excess to inside of container and glue in place. Cut slit measuring 1 inch x ³⁄₁₆ inch in the middle of the bottom of container. Cut two scraps of fabric 1 inch x ½ inch and glue in place on each side of slit opening, ¼ inch extending inside and ¼ inch extending outside opening. Cover slit with free-form felt shape to hide two glued fabric scraps. Cut a slit in felt to fit slit in container. Cover remaining surface of cap with various free-form felt pieces, using photo as guide. To put top and bottom together, simply snap lid onto container.

Owl Bank from Margarine Tub

For all the people you know who collect owls.

Materials:

1 round margarine tub
Newspaper
White tacky glue
Acrylic paints (we've used ivory, white, light brown, dark brown, and mustard)
Brown antiquing spray
Soft cloth
Compass
Lightweight cardboard

Instructions:

Cut a slit in side of tub ⅜ inch x 1¼ inches. Tear newspaper into strips approximately 1½ inches long and ½ inch wide. Glue strips to outside of tub, and to lid and rim, overlapping to give texture. Let dry. Paint over newspaper with ivory acrylic paint. Using pattern as guide, cut ears, eyes, beak, and wings from cardboard. Paint ears dark brown, eyes dark brown with black centers, and beak and wings light brown. Let dry. Using photo as guide, glue ears, eyes, beak, and wings in place (ears go one on each side of slit). Let dry. Paint feathers on front bottom half of lid by dabbing paint on in alternating colors: ivory, light brown, dark brown, white, and mustard. Let dry. Antique container by spraying with brown antiquing spray and wiping immediately with a soft cloth. To keep tub from rolling, cut 4-inch circle from cardboard, then cut cardboard circle in half. Paint half circle dark brown. Let dry. Glue to bottom of tub so that it will lie flat to form a base, with rounded edge forward.

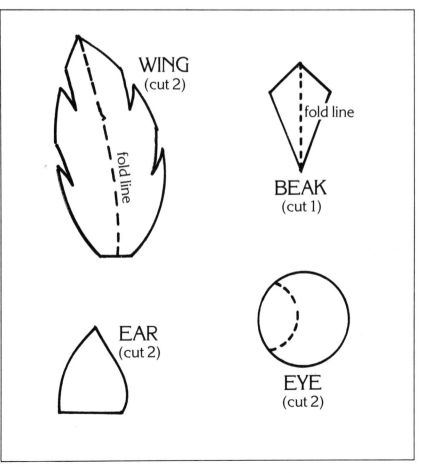

WING
(cut 2)

fold line

BEAK
(cut 1)

fold line

EAR
(cut 2)

EYE
(cut 2)

Trivets from Bottle Caps

Watermelon Trivet

Materials:

Thin cardboard or illustration
    board 7" x 12"
24 bottle caps
White tacky glue
Red acrylic paint
Felt scraps; red, dark green, and
    white
Permanent fine-line black
    marking pen

Instructions:

Cut watermelon shape from cardboard, using pattern as guide. Paint bottle caps red. Set aside to dry. Glue red felt to each side of cardboard. Trim to cardboard shape. Cut ½-inch strip of dark green felt, using pattern as guide. Glue green felt to edge of watermelon shape. Cut ¼-inch strip of white felt, using pattern as guide. Glue on top of green felt along inner edge (see photograph). Glue bottle caps to watermelon shape as shown in photograph, spacing evenly. Let dry. Mark seed shapes on bottle caps with permanent black marking pen.

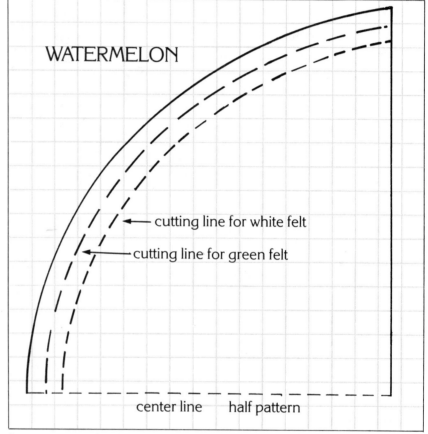

WATERMELON

← cutting line for white felt

← cutting line for green felt

center line   half pattern

1 square equals ⁵/₁₆ inch

Apple Trivet

Materials:

Thin cardboard or illustration
    board 7" x 7"
13 bottle caps
Red acrylic paint
Felt scraps: red and light green
White tacky glue

Instructions:

Cut apple shape from cardboard, using pattern as guide. Paint bottle caps red. Set aside to dry. Glue red felt to each side of cardboard. Trim to cardboard shape. Glue two pieces of light green felt, each measuring 3½ inches x 3 inches, together. Transfer leaf pattern to felt and cut out. Glue leaves to top edge of apple. Glue bottle caps to apple shape as shown in photograph, spacing evenly.

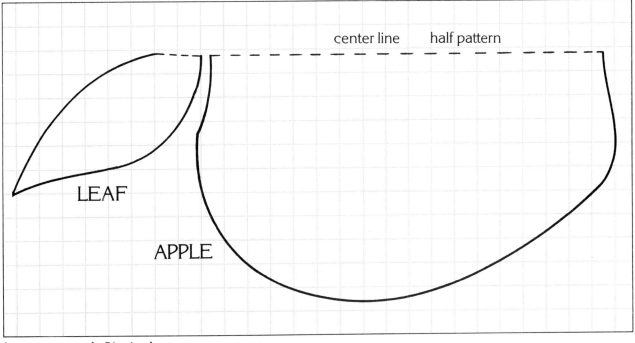

center line   half pattern

LEAF

APPLE

1 square equals ⁵/₁₆ inch

Strawberry Baskets

Hang one of these baskets on Mother's door in honor of the May Day tradition.

Flower-Covered Strawberry Basket

Materials:

Art paper: green, yellow, red, orange, and pink
Strawberry basket
Paper hole puncher
2 chenille stems (any of the above colors)
1 yd. ribbon coordinated with art paper for trim
White tacky glue

Instructions:

Cut four pieces of green art paper 1½ inches x 3¾ inches each. Snip strips of paper at intervals approximately 1/16 inch to 1/8 inch apart, and ¾ inch to 1 inch in length, tapered at top, to create grass. Glue grass around bottom outside edge of strawberry basket. Punch holes from yellow, red, orange, and pink paper. Glue five "holes" in a circle together onto side of basket to form flower. Glue a contrasting circle in center. Glue flowers at various spots on all four sides of basket. Refer to photo as guide for placement. *To make handle,* twist the two chenille stems together and bend 1 inch from each end. Attach each end of chenille stem to sides of basket by bringing bent end through open work in side of basket and bending up around rim and back to chenille, twisting to hold. Glue in place. Repeat process on other side. Tie ribbons to each side to help hold ends of chenille while glue is drying and as decoration. Wrap ribbon around handle as shown in photograph, if desired. Glue ribbon ends to chenille handle behind bows.

Fabric-Covered Strawberry Basket

Materials:

Fabric scraps
Strawberry basket
1 piece 18-gauge wire, 12″ long
White tacky glue
Rickrack trim

Instructions:

Cut fabric to fit bottom of basket, adding ½ inch all around. Glue fabric to bottom of basket, gluing excess up sides. Cut fabric to fit sides, adding ½ inch all around. Glue fabric to sides, folding raw edges under and gluing in place to hold (see photograph). *To make handle,* cut a strip of fabric 2 inches x 11 inches. Glue wire down center of wrong side of fabric. Fold ends of strip over ½ inch and fold each edge to center. Glue in place. Bend wire to form handle and glue ends to inside of basket. Glue rickrack to outside top edge of basket and to outside of handle.

Snail Tape Dispenser

Materials:

Plastic foam ball 1½″ diameter
Tape dispenser for body
Green acrylic paint
2 paper hole punchers, large and small
Art paper scraps: black, white, green, yellow, orange, and hot pink
White tacky glue
Black thread

Instructions:

To give shape to snail's head, slightly indent foam ball in cheek area, using pattern as guide. Paint head and tape dispenser green. Let dry. Punch two large circles from white art paper and two small ones from black for eyes. Glue in place. Using patterns as guides, cut eyelashes, nose, and feelers from black art paper and glue in place. Let dry. Glue thread onto head for mouth, as shown in drawing. Glue head to tape dispenser body as shown in photograph. Let dry. Cut three large leaves from green paper.

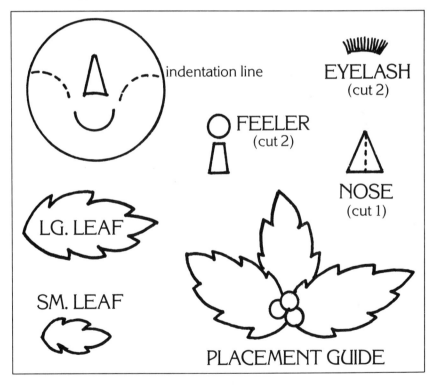

Glue circles of various colors punched with a paper hole puncher onto middle of the three leaves to form a flower. Cut two small leaves from green paper.

Glue in place at neckline as shown in photograph. Glue paper punched dots of various colors to sides of tape dispenser in flower patterns.

Pie Tin Thread and Pin Holder

A quick and inexpensive bazaar item, easy to sell because it's so functional: The lid holds pins and thread is stored inside.

Materials:

Felt scraps: hot pink, red, light green, and beige
Aluminum foil pie tin 5″ diameter
Compass
Plastic foam ball 4½″ diameter (use top ⅓ only) for lid
White tacky glue
Lightweight cardboard
Pinking shears
Polyester fiberfill
Needle and thread

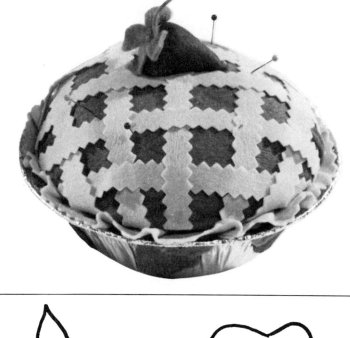

Instructions:

Using pattern as guide, cut three red and three hot pink flat strawberries from felt. Cut six small hulls from light green felt. Glue strawberries on outside of tin, alternating red and hot pink strawberries and spacing evenly. Glue hulls above each strawberry. *To make lid:* cut a circle 6½ inches in diameter from hot pink felt. Cut top third from plastic foam ball, coat with glue, and place felt on top, smoothing to fit ball. Glue excess felt to underside of ball, clipping felt so it lies flat. Cut a circle 4 inches in diameter from cardboard. Cover one side with hot pink felt, gluing in place. Trim felt to size of cardboard. Glue felt-covered circle to bottom of plastic foam ball. Using pinking shears, cut two strips, each ¾ inch x 12 inches, from beige felt. Tuck felt strip every inch to form gathers. Glue strips along bottom edge of ball, extending strip ⅜ inch out from edge. With pinking shears, cut ten strips each measuring ⅜ inch x 6½ inches from beige felt. Place strips on top of plastic foam ball and weave to form pastry shell, using photo as guide for placement and spacing.

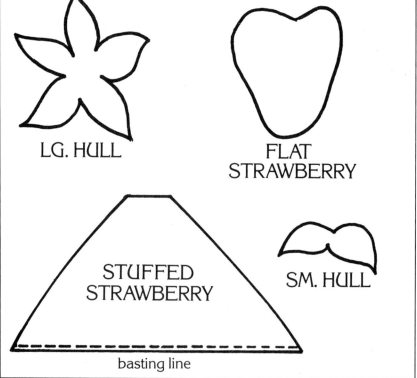

LG. HULL

FLAT STRAWBERRY

STUFFED STRAWBERRY

SM. HULL

basting line

Glue strips in place, cutting excess off at edge of ball. Cut stuffed strawberry from red felt and large hull from green felt, using pattern as guide. Baste top of strawberry with needle and thread. Do not gather stitches yet. Place a small piece of fiberfill in center of strawberry. Roll felt over fiberfill to form a cone. Glue sides together. Pull basting stitch to gather at top to form strawberry. Tie off securely. Glue hull in place on top of strawberry. Glue strawberry to top of pie as shown in photograph. Place pie top on tin.

116

CHAPTER EIGHT

Brown-Bag Bewitchery

This chapter describes uses for one of our favorite materials—the common, everyday, no-cost-to-you grocer's paper sack. It's in the bag (and in this chapter): how to make a stunning wreath, paint Scandinavian-type ornaments from double thicknesses, do quilling, and—perhaps the most spectacular use of all—create designs that look like metal. Be careful; brown bags can spellbind you to such a degree that you'll never ever throw one away.

Natural Wreath from Brown Bags

Materials:

Plastic foam wreath 12″ diameter
Brown bags
White tacky glue
Straight pins
10 pieces 18-gauge bare wire, 18″
   each
25 pieces 22-gauge bare wire, 8″
   each
Wire cutters
1 roll brown ½″ florist's tape
Several small pinecones
Seed pods of eucalyptus, maple,
   etc.
Hammer and small nail
Small pieces of driftwood
   (optional)
1 chenille stem for hanger

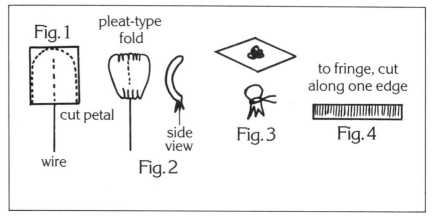

Instructions:

To cover foam wreath, cut nine strips of brown bag 2 inches wide x 14 to 16 inches long. Attach to wreath by wrapping around and around; secure with glue and pins. Make sure strips cover all of wreath. Do not leave any exposed areas. Set aside to dry.

There are two basic flowers on the wreath, the large poppy focal flowers and the small fantasy flowers. *To make poppies,* you will need five double-thickness petals for each flower. For each petal, glue two thicknesses brown grocery bag 4 inches x 3½ inches together with an 8-inch piece of 22-gauge wire down the center, Fig. 1. Following drawing, cut five petals. Shaping of petals must be done while glued petal is still damp and "setting up." To shape petal, simply pinch "flute" folds at top and bottom edges as shown in Fig. 2. At this time you must also bend wire to curve petal. Set the five petals aside to dry. Repeat procedure to make two more poppies. While petals are drying, assemble the poppy centers. *To make center,* cut a 5-inch square (single thickness) of brown bag. Place some scraps of

brown grocery bag (scraps cut off from petals) into center of square. Wrap square piece around scraps, Fig. 3, and wire tightly with 22-gauge wire to form ball shape. Cut off excess bag below wire. *To make stamen,* cut a strip of brown grocery bag 2½ inches x 14 inches. Fringe-cut one edge 1½ inches down, 1/16 inch apart, all the way across, Fig. 4. Glue fringed piece to back of poppy "ball" center. Let dry. *To assemble poppies,* apply small amount of glue along bottom edge of petals. Place petals evenly around poppy center. You might find it easier to wire two or three petals to center first, then add remaining petals. Allow flowers to dry upside down "on their faces" to help prevent petals from sliding down stem. When dry, tape stems with brown florist's tape.

To make fantasy flowers: There are two different types. The first is a single strip of brown grocery bag 2 inches x 16 inches with fringe cut on one edge, 1½ inches down, 1/16 inch apart. Apply line of glue along uncut edge. Roll to form flower. When glue is dry, fluff fringe outward. Outside row of fringe may be slightly folded for added texture.

The second fantasy flower resembles a chrysanthemum. To make flower, cut strip of brown grocery bag 4 inches x 6 inches

and fold in half lengthwise. Fringe-cut on folded edge, 1½ inches down, 1/16 inch apart. Unfold and apply line of glue on uncut edges. Refold and glue edges together. Place another line of glue along uncut edge and roll to form flower. Let dry. Some variations have stamens added. *To make stamens,* simply fringe a 1¼ inch x 3 inch strip of brown bag. Apply a line of glue to unfringed edge and roll. Glue into center of fantasy flower.

For each wheat spray, cut an 8-inch length of 18-gauge wire and wrap it with florist's tape. Cut strip of brown bag 1 inch x 8 inches. Fringe along one edge, ¾ inch down, 1/16 inch apart. Apply line of glue along unfringed edge. Starting at top of taped wire, wrap strip around and around, slightly overlapping each row. Use caution not to put excess glue on fringed area as fringe will not fluff out as well if soiled with glue.

To attach poppies to wreath, cut wires to about 1 inch. Before inserting into foam, evenly space poppies around wreath. Dip wire into glue and push into wreath. (Note: Because you have already covered the wreath with brown grocery bag, it may be difficult to stick the wires through, so use a sharp object such as a nail to make holes first.) Next, wire

three pinecones to three sprays of wheat with 22-gauge wire. Tape stem with brown florist's tape. Glue into wreath around poppies. Using photo as guide for placement, fill in space between poppies with the small fantasy flowers and white pinecones and seed pods. *To attach fantasy flowers,* apply glue to bottom of flower and attach to wreath with straight pins. *To attach pinecones,* wire with 22-gauge wire and cover wire with brown tape. Dip wire into glue and insert into foam wreath. *To attach pods* with stems, tape a 22-gauge wire to stem, dip in glue, and insert into wreath. If pods do not have stem, gently hammer small nail into pod to make hole, glue a taped 18-gauge wire into hole, dip wire into glue, and insert into wreath. Small pieces of driftwood may also be wired or glued onto wreath to fill in any open spots. *To hang wreath,* fold chenille stem in half, dip ends in glue, and push ends into back of foam wreath, forming a loop.

Brown-Bag
Flower Arrangement

Materials:

Brown bags
White tacky glue
About 10 pieces 18-gauge wire,
   18" each
About 25 pieces 22-gauge wire,
   12" each
Brown ½" florist's tape
Basket, or wide-mouthed vase or
   jar
Ribbon for trim (optional)
Plastic foam base, 3" x 4"
Dried baby's breath
Pinecones
Florist's clay

Instructions:

By simply following the directions for the flowers and wheat sprays in the Natural Wreath from Brown Bags (page 118), or making your own variations, you can create an arrangement of brown bag flowers. Use a basket or vase, or cover a jar with a paper bag and tie a ribbon around it. Arrange flowers in place by sticking wires into a plastic foam base. Wrap baby's breath and pinecones with 22-gauge wire. Attach to 18-gauge wire for strength by wrapping 22-gauge wire around 18-gauge. Wrap stems with florist's tape and stick into foam base. Anchor the foam base in the container with air-drying florist's clay.

Brown-Bag Quilled Ornaments

Quilling, or paper filigree—both terms in use two hundred years ago by the Colonial ladies who practiced the craft—requires strips of paper fluted, folded, curled, rolled, pinched, or coiled, and placed on end in rows so as to bear some resemblance (often only a faint one) to a row of quills. The technique was used for ornamenting the borders of flower or shell plaques. Our technique is a simplified version of this highly developed old craft, but it produces enchanting, no-cost, quick and easy decorations. String quilled ornaments on the Christmas tree, affix them to a gift package, or hang several together and make a mobile that—when light passes through—is reminiscent of filigree work.

Materials:

Brown bags
Clear plastic or clear food wrap
White tacky glue
Fine gold cord for hanger

Instructions:

Cut strips of bag 1 inch wide. Fold strips in half lengthwise and glue together to form double thickness. Place pattern (ours or your own design) on flat surface and cover with sheet of clear plastic. Secure plastic and pattern to table to avoid slipping. Roll quilling strips to desired shapes and sizes to fill pattern (see photograph). Glue quilled pieces together at sides to form desired shape. (Excess glue will attach to plastic but project can be pulled off easily when completed.) Let dry. Remove ornament from plastic and tie or glue gold cord to top for hanger.

Quilling can also be done on paper to make cards, ornaments, etc. Glue quilled pieces together at sides and then to paper surfaces.

1 square equals 7/16 inch

122

Painted Ornaments
on Brown Bags

(See photo on page 123.)

A quick and inexpensive shortcut to the real Scandinavian designs.

Materials:

Brown bags
Pinking shears (optional)
White tacky glue
Acrylic paint: red, white, and
  green
Paper hole punchers, small and
  regular sizes
Fine gold cord for hangers

Instructions:

Using patterns as guides, cut designs from brown bags. Cut some with pinking shears for an interesting edge. Glue three thicknesses of brown bag together where indicated on pattern. Let dry. Using small and regular paper punchers, punch ornaments where indicated on pattern. To paint designs on ornaments, use the handle of a fine brush, dipping end into paint and dotting on designs. Use fine brush end for leaves and scrolls. Glue cord to backs of ornaments for hanger, or punch a hole and tie cord through.

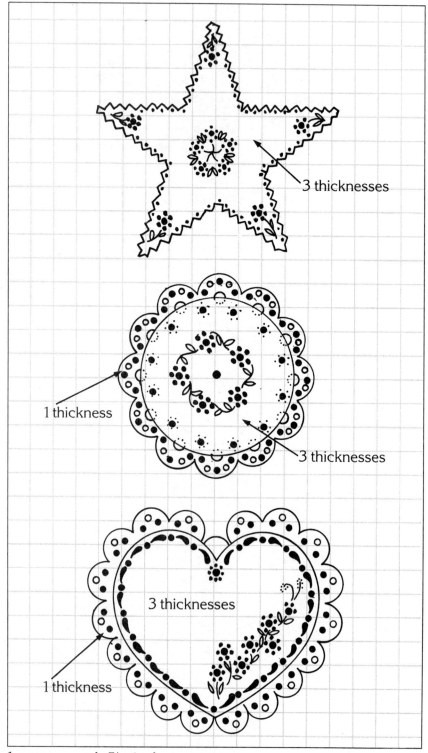

3 thicknesses

1 thickness

3 thicknesses

3 thicknesses

1 thickness

1 square equals 7/16 inch

BURNED BROWN BAG SCULPTURE

Metal sculpture is popular and expensive. With brown bags and the burning process described below, you can create your own magnificent sculptures, surprisingly like the very high-priced ones. When polished and shined, the brown-bag designs have the feel of metal, and are extremely durable yet very light-weight.

How to Burn Brown Bags for a Metallic Look

1. You'll be working with fire, so take every sensible precaution. Be sure all flammable materials are covered and out of the way. Work outdoors or in a well-ventilated area on a table covered with aluminum foil. Keep a fire extinguisher handy.

2. Transfer your design to a brown paper bag. Brush a heavy coat of white tacky glue over the design (on one side of the paper only), and immediately hold the glued design over a candle flame, rotating it so that the flame touches every part but doesn't burn a hole in it. The bag will not catch fire as long as it's well coated with glue—the glue itself is not flammable. Hold the design as low as possible without snuffing out the candle. A pair of long tongs might be helpful with some projects to keep your fingers as far from the flame as possible. Continue rotating design over the flame for one and a half to two minutes, until it looks very black and sooty. (If you prefer, rotate design ½ inch to 1 inch above flame instead; however, it will take a little longer to blacken the design and the surface will remain smoother since the heat from the flame will not bubble the surface.)

3. Now test whether or not it is done: Take a soft cloth or cleansing tissue and lightly wipe away the soot. If, under the soot, all surfaces are black and metallic looking, you are finished. If some brown paper still shows, continue to burn it for another half minute or so, then wipe away soot and check once again. When the design is black all over, clean off soot, let cool, dry, and harden.

Brown-Bag Autumn Leaves

Materials:

Brown bags
18-gauge wire, 6″ for each leaf
White tacky glue
Candle
Gold antiquing paste
Cardboard or illustration board
   covered with fabric for
   background (optional)
Dried branch (optional)
Frame (optional)

Instructions:

Cut leaves from double thickness of brown bag; glue together with wire in between, using pattern as guide. Make seven leaves, or amount needed for your own design (an odd number is best). Now read and follow the three steps on How to Burn Brown Bags for a Metallic Look, page 125. When leaves are completely dry, antique them as described in the Brown-Bag Sculptured Horse, page 127. Glue the leaves to the background board, guided by photo for placement or following your own design. We show the leaves on a manzanita branch and in a frame. Any dried branch, cut to fit the background and secured to it with wire from behind, could be used. Or the leaves could be arranged by themselves, without a branch. The leaves could also be arranged on the homemade paper described on page 19. Frame is optional.

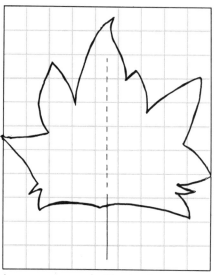

1 square equals 8/16 inch

Brown-Bag Sculptured Horse

Materials:

Cardboard
2 pieces 18-gauge wire, each 5″
   long
Black acrylic paint
Florist's tape ½″ wide
Large brown bag
White tacky glue
Candle
Gold antiquing paste
Block of wood 2″ x 4″ x 8″ for
   stand
Drill
Sandpaper
Optional wood finishes: stains,
   varnishes, wax

Instructions:

For body of horse, cut shape from cardboard following pattern. Cover wires with florist's tape and paint with black acrylic paint. Let dry. Glue wires in place on one side of cardboard, using pattern as guide. Glue one thickness of bag to one side of cardboard and cut the bag to match the card-board. Repeat on opposite side. Let dry. Now read and follow the three steps in How to Burn Brown Bags for a Metallic Look, page 125. When horse is dry, add highlights with gold antiquing paste. Apply with fingers to all raised surfaces, leaving plenty of black area for the metallic look. To avoid overantiquing, apply paste lightly at first; more can be added later if desired, but it can't be re-moved if you've put on too much. It's best to dip your fingers in the paste and wipe the excess off on a cloth before applying.

To make stand: Drill two holes approximately 1½ inches deep in block of wood for horse wires. Sand the raw edges of the wood and either leave the wood natural or finish it with stain, varnish, or wax. Insert wires of horse into holes in stand.

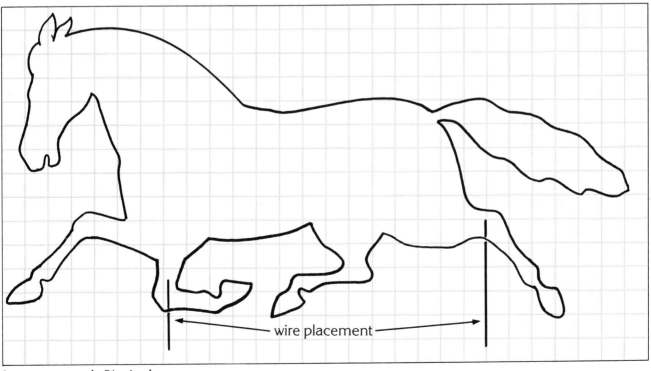

wire placement

1 square equals ⁵/₁₆ inch

Brown-Bag Butterfly Sculpture

Materials:

Brown bag
10 pieces 18-gauge wire, 12″ each
Florist's tape 12″ wide
Black acrylic paint
White tacky glue
Candle
Gold antiquing paste
1 small piece driftwood
Drill

Instructions:

For each butterfly, glue two 3-inch squares of brown bag together with wire between (see pattern). Trace butterfly pattern onto square and cut. Make three butterflies. Now follow the three steps on How to Burn Brown Bags for a Metallic Look, page 125. When dry, apply gold antiquing paste with your fingers to raised surfaces. *For flower,* glue two 2-inch squares of brown bag together with wire in between. Trace petal pattern onto square and cut. Make five petals. *For leaf,* glue two 3 inch x 2 inch pieces of brown bag together with wire between. Trace leaf pattern onto bag and cut. Make two leaves. Again, follow the directions for burning brown bags and use gold antiquing paste to highlight. Tape wire on each piece with florist's tape and paint with black acrylic paint. Let dry. Cut two feelers for each butterfly, following pattern. Paint with black acrylic paint. Let dry. Glue feelers in place on butterfly heads (see photograph). *To assemble flower,* bend wires at petal's base. Tape the five petals together with florist's tape, following guide for placement. Tape two leaves in place on flower stem. Paint wires black. Let dry. Cut wires on butterflies to varied lengths—7 inches, 5 inches, 3 inches—to balance arrangement. Cut stem wire on flower to approximately 1½ inches. Drill holes approximately 1½ inches deep in driftwood for butterflies, leaves, and flower, following photo as a guide for placement or making your own design. Insert wires into holes in driftwood.

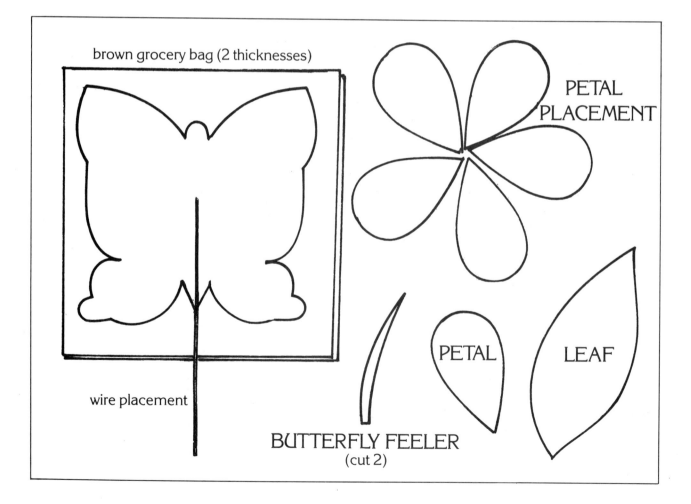

brown grocery bag (2 thicknesses)

wire placement

PETAL PLACEMENT

PETAL

LEAF

BUTTERFLY FEELER
(cut 2)

CHAPTER NINE

Super-Simple Money-Saver Youth Projects

All the projects given in these pages are moneysavers—most of them simple enough to be done at one sitting—and there's no "science" separating the projects that could be done by young people as compared to those meant only for adults. So why this separate chapter for children filled with "recipes" for using materials that are organized by type elsewhere in this book?

It's because the need for youth-oriented material is so very great. Over the years in which one or the other of us has done our own TV shows, demonstrated to the public at fairs and other large gatherings, or written up craft projects for magazines and newspapers, the one need that seems always with us is the need youth leaders have, year in and year out, for design ideas. By youth leaders we mean teachers, scout leaders, camp counselors, children's librarians, editors of young-teen magazines, social workers who deal with kids, and even—or especially—parents.

So here is our collection—collected with some trepidation for we have had to be so arbitrary—of super-simple, money-saver projects for young people to make from "scraps" and found objects. (We have not included directions for any of the photogenic little dolls and animal figures made from plastic foam eggs and decorated with all kinds of hats, ribbons, and painted-on features, because children are always imaginative enough to create these on their own. But we do want to remind you that they are popular.)

Burlap Notepad Holder

Materials:

1 yd. 2½" wide ribbon
White tacky glue
1 yd. 5" wide burlap ribbon
Macrame ring 3" diameter
½ yd. rickrack trim
Pen or pencil
Small notepad, approx. 4" x 6"

Instructions:

Glue the ribbon down middle of burlap. Cut the glued-together ribbons into three pieces: a 14-inch length, a 12-inch length, and a 3-inch length. Fold end of 12-inch length to a point. Bring point through macrame ring, fold over, and glue end to back, holding macrame ring in place. *For pencil loop,* fold the 3-inch length in half and glue cut edges together. Glue loop to 12-inch length, 4 inches from top. Glue rickrack over top edge of loop. *For notepad loop,* fold the remaining 14-inch length in half and glue cut edges together. Glue loop 1 inch below bottom of pencil loop. Glue rickrack over top edge of notepad loop to finish. Insert pad and pencil or pen.

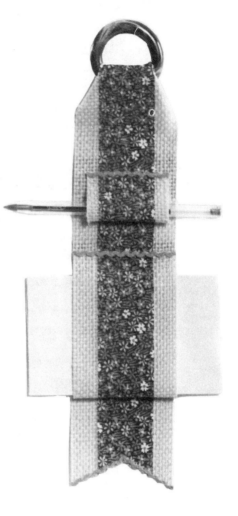

Burlap Calendar

Materials:

6½" x 14" piece burlap
2 pieces braid trim, each 7½" long
Silk flowers for trimming
1 plain calendar about 3" x 4"
2 wooden beads ⅜"–⅝" diameter
Dowel stick, 6½" length
   (diameter to fit into beads)
Fine gold cord for hanging

Instructions:

Fold burlap in half crosswise. Glue the two layers of burlap together, leaving ½ inch at fold unglued to form a channel in which later to insert dowel for hanger. Be sure to spread glue to all edges, as burlap will be cut to size and glue keeps it from unraveling. Let dry. Cut burlap to measure 6 inches x 6½ inches. Glue braid trim along side edges, folding excess over to back side at both top and bottom edges, and glue to hold in place. Glue silk flowers and calendar in place. Insert dowel stick into channel. Glue wooden beads to ends. Tie gold cord to dowel for hanger.

Milk Carton Bookends

Materials:

2 quart-size waxed cardboard milk cartons
White tacky glue
Plaster of paris
Strips of paper towels
Rickrack and lace trimmings
Acrylic paints: white for windows and curtains, brown for roof, light blue for house, dark blue for trim
Brown antiquing spray
Soft cloth
Spray varnish

Instructions:

Cut bottom off milk cartons to desired height and discard. Glue spout closed. Turn cartons upside down and fill with plaster of paris, following directions on package. Let plaster dry completely. Glue paper towels to all outside surfaces of milk cartons to give cartons texture. Let dry. Draw design on milk cartons, using pattern as guide, or design your own pattern. Glue trim in place. Paint design. Let dry. Antique with brown antiquing spray by spraying a small section at a time and wiping immediately with a soft cloth. Seal outside surfaces with spray varnish.

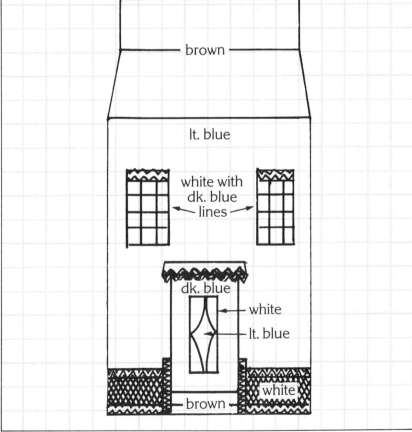

brown

lt. blue

white with dk. blue lines

dk. blue

white

lt. blue

brown

white

1 square equals 5/16 inch

133

Felt Owl Magnet

(See photo on page 115.)

Materials:

2 moving eyes, 12 mm.
Felt scraps: brown, yellow, and
   orange
Pinking shears
White tacky glue
Small magnet or magnet tape
3 sequins

Instructions:

Cut owl pieces following patterns, using brown felt for body, orange for wings and beak, and yellow for breast piece. (When cutting wings, cut curved edges with pinking shears.) Following photo, glue wings and breast piece on body. Glue eyes and beak in place on face. Glue sequins on breast piece. Glue magnet to back of owl.

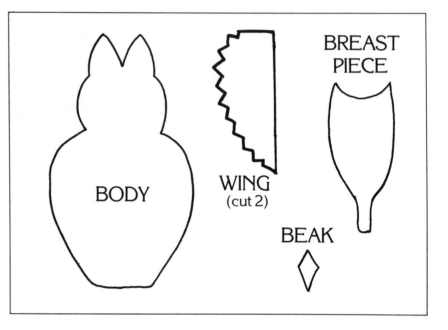

BODY

WING
(cut 2)

BREAST PIECE

BEAK

Peach-Pit Chicken

A nectarine, plum, or other fruit pit of the approximate size of the peach pit would do fine.

Materials:

Wooden toothpick
Yellow acrylic paint
1 peach pit
Yellow or white cloth pom-pom
⅟₄ inch diameter
White tacky glue
2 black seed beads

Instructions:

Paint toothpick yellow. Let dry. Glue pom-pom to pit. For beak, snip ⅟₁₆ inch from end of toothpick and glue to pom-pom. For eyes, glue two seed beads onto pom-pom above beak.

Spoon Mouse with Sucker

Materials:

Felt scraps for ears and cheeks
White tacky glue
Plastic spoon
Narrow ribbon for trim (optional)
Black beads for eyes (optional)
Permanent fine-line black
    marking pen
White or black thread for
    whiskers
1 seed bead
1 Tootsie Roll sucker
Wide ribbon for holding sucker to
    spoon

Instructions:

To make ears, cut felt in contrasting colors, using pattern as guide. Glue ears together as shown in photograph. Glue ears to top edge of spoon. Glue small bow of narrow ribbon between ears, if desired. *To make eyes,* glue black beads in middle of back of spoon, or mark eyes on spoon with pen. *For whiskers,* cut five 1-inch lengths of thread and glue in place below eyes. *For nose,* glue seed bead in center of thread whiskers. Draw mouth on with pen. Cut small hearts from felt for cheeks and glue in place as shown. Tie sucker onto spoon with ribbon, tying bow in front.

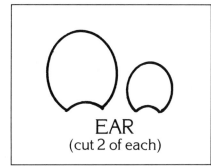

EAR
(cut 2 of each)

Paper-Punched Cards

Materials:

Art paper scraps in assorted
  colors
Paper hole punchers, small and
  regular size
White tacky glue
Permanent fine-line black
  marking pen (optional)
Scalloped-edged scissors and
  pinking shears (optional)

Instructions:

Cut art paper to desired sizes
for cards. Punch holes from various colors of art paper. Using
patterns and photos as guides for
placement or following your own
design, glue punched holes on
card, overlapping circles to make
desired shapes. Further decorate
card by punching out holes from
background, trimming the edges
with pinking or scalloped-edged
shears, inking in details, gluing
on other art paper shapes, and the
like.

137

Button Cards and Ornaments

(See photo on page 137.)

Materials:

Art paper in assorted colors
Jar lids
Felt scraps in assorted colors
White tacky glue
Permanent marking pens in assorted colors, or acrylic paints
Paper hole puncher (optional)
Pinking and scalloped-edged shears (optional)
Buttons in various sizes and colors
Optional trimmings: thread for whiskers, cotton fiberfill for beards and hats, ribbon, braid, rickrack
Narrow ribbon for hangers

Instructions:

To make cards, cut art paper to desired size for card. Mark paper lightly for pattern placement, using our patterns or creating your own. Glue background items on first (e.g., paper punches, paper shapes). Glue buttons in place. Add detail with marking pens or paint. Glue on additional trim, if desired.

To make jar lid ornaments, line inside of lid with felt or art paper, or paint with acrylic paint. Glue on background items, then buttons. Add detail with marking pens or paint, then glue on additional details. Glue braid around edge of lid if desired, and glue on a loop of ribbon for hanger.

Airplane from Gum and Candy

Materials:

1 stick gum
Small scrap felt (optional)
1 package Smarties candies (or
    similar roll of small candies)
1 small rubber band
2 Lifesavers candies
Yarn for hanger

Instructions:

To make airplane, replace outside paper on gum wrapper with felt if desired. Referring to pattern as guide for placement of candy, slip end of rubber band over end of gum and slide to middle of stick of gum. Take the loose end of the rubber band that is hanging down and slip it through the middle of one Lifesaver, over Smarties candy package, and through the middle of other Lifesaver and bring end of rubber band around other end of stick of gum. This will hold airplane together. Tie yarn to rubber band loops on top of wings for hanger.

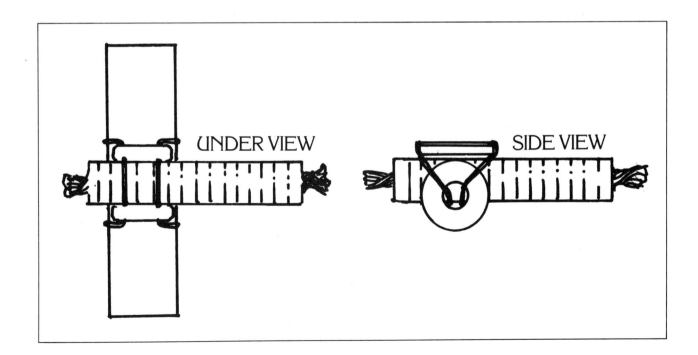

UNDER VIEW

SIDE VIEW

Cookie Cutter Ornaments

Materials:

Cookie cutters in various shapes
Fabric scraps
White tacky glue
Acrylic paint (optional)
Gold braid, rickrack, or lace trim
Miniature wooden figures
    (optional)
Optional trimmings: dried flower
    sprays, cotton, ribbon, etc.
Gold cord for hanger

Instructions:

Paint cookie cutters or cover with fabric. Trim outside edges with braid, rickrack, or lace trim. Arrangements can be made inside the cookie cutters by gluing in dried materials and miniature figurines as shown in the photograph. Trim top of cookie cutter, if desired. Tie or glue hanger to top.

Margarine Container and Tin Can Ornaments

Materials:

Small round margarine
   container or tin can
Felt scraps
Acrylic paint (optional)
Gold braid
Greeting cards
White tacky glue
Optional trimmings: dried
   flowers, ribbon scraps, angel
   hair, sequins, beads
Gold cord for hanger

Instructions:

For margarine container: Discard lid. Cover outside with felt, or paint if desired. Glue gold braid around rim, as shown in photograph. Cut figures from greeting card and glue onto base. Glue angel hair or dried materials around card figures. Trim sides of inside of container with sequins or beads as shown. Trim top (outside) as desired. Glue on gold cord for hanger.

For tin can: Remove both ends from can. Cover inside and outside with felt, gluing in place. Glue gold braid around front rim. Cut greeting card to fit back of can and glue in place. For a three-dimensional effect, cut figures from remaining piece of card (or another card) and glue to base of can, as shown in photograph. Add trimmings to inside and top of can as desired. Glue on gold cord for hanger.

Christmas Angels

Materials (for one angel):

1 large Christmas card
White tacky glue
Gold braid, sequins, glitter, gold cord, pearls, ribbon for trimming
4″ wire-centered gold cord for halo
Fine gold cord for hanger (optional)

Instructions:

Cut two angels from card, one in reverse, using pattern as guide. Slit one figure down to dot on pattern, using dotted line as a guide. Slit the other one up to dot on pattern using straight line as a guide. Work the bottom slit down through the top slit. The angel will be four-sided. Lay angel flat. Glue bodies together from head to bottom of skirt along slit. Fold the wings back and the arms toward the front. Bend both sides of body back, making a crease down the center. Bend top of angel forward slightly at waist. This makes a V-shaped front so that angel will stand. *To form halo:* Wrap wire-centered cord around a jar or other cylinder approximately 1 inch in diameter, twist ends together, and bend ends down at top of twist. Glue wire to back of angel's head. Decorate angel with gold braid, sequins, pearls, glitter for glamor. Glue on gold cord for hanger, if desired.

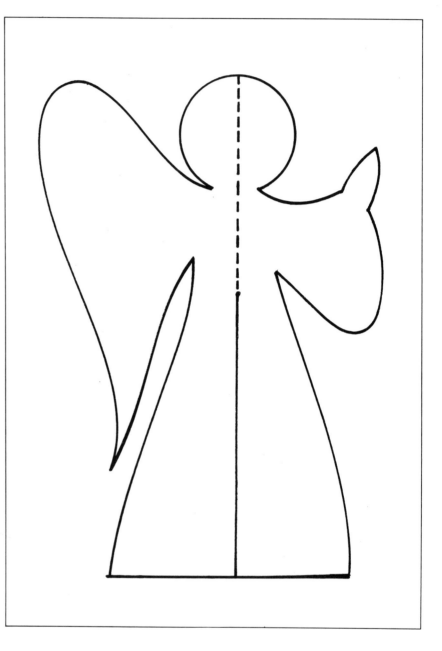

CHAPTER TEN

Super-Special Party Designs

Even a simple party becomes important when it includes an attractively set table, but because this chapter features dramatic designs for those big occasions which people always celebrate with some formality and sense of tradition, we call it super-special. You'll find here a bridal-shower centerpiece, a lovely way to announce some important news, a design for a money tree honoring a silver anniversary, and a Three Wise Men sculpture to use on your table (or mantel) all through the Christmas season. We've also included an endearing clown in a gay setting that will delight not only the young 'uns but guests of all ages at a very-special-child's party. Every child will feel very special with such a birthday centerpiece.

Bridal Shower Centerpiece

Can you think of a lovelier centerpiece for a formal bridal shower than this elegance?

Materials:

2 paper doilies 8″ diameter
18-gauge covered wire: two 12″
  lengths, one 5″ length
White ½″ florist's tape
White tacky glue
1 yd. 2″-wide eyelet lace
Straight pins
Stapler
Plastic foam disc 1″ x 6″
26-gauge covered wire, two 12″
  lengths
Lace fabric for butterfly
4″ piece chenille stem
3 white satin multi-looped bows
  (see instructions page 158)

Instructions:

To make umbrellas: Cut pie-shaped wedge from each doily. Glue edges together, overlapping ¼ inch to create umbrella shape. Wrap the two 12-inch lengths of 18-gauge wire with florist's tape. Carefully punch ends of taped wires through top underside points of umbrellas. Glue in place to hold. Set aside to dry. *To make base:* Pleat lace every 2 inches and staple together to hold. Glue and pin lace trim to top of foam disc, 1 inch from edge. *To make butterfly:* Bend one 12-inch length of 26-gauge wire to shape of butterfly, using pattern as guide. Glue wire down to lace fabric and let set flat until glue is dry. Cut excess lace away from outside of wire. *To make head of butterfly,* twist 1 inch of chenille stem around pencil and glue remainder of stem down middle of butterfly. Bend 5-inch length of 18-gauge wire 1 inch from end. Glue bent end to bottom side of butterfly. Let glue dry. *To assemble centerpiece:* Dip wired ends of satin multi-looped bows into glue, then insert into base. Fill in around bows with silk flowers and greenery. Stick doily umbrellas and butterfly into middle of base as shown in photograph.

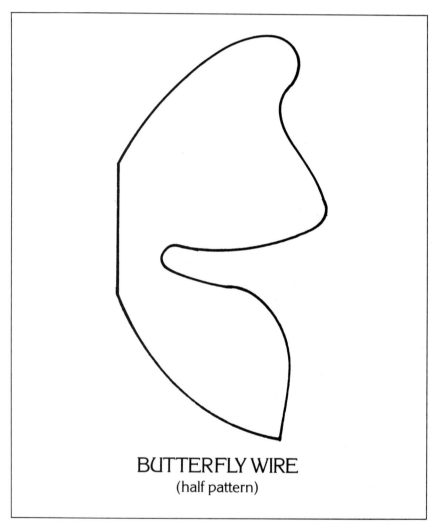

BUTTERFLY WIRE
(half pattern)

Baby Shower Centerpiece

Materials:

1 quart-size plastic bleach bottle
    for buggy
Gingham fabric scraps
White tacky glue
Lace trim
2 pieces 18-gauge covered wire,
    18″ each
White ½″ florist's tape
Needle-nosed pliers
Lightweight cardboard
White acrylic paint
2 plastic foam bases: 1″ x 6″ x 12″
    and 1″ x 5″ x 6″
3 yds. nylon tulle ribbon, 6″ wide
20 pieces 26-gauge wire, 12″ each
3 wooden toothpicks
6 yds. ribbon for bows and trim
Silk flowers and greenery
    for trim

Instructions:

Cut two pieces of baby buggy
from bleach bottle, following pattern. Cut fabric to fit outside surface of cut pieces, adding ½ inch
all around edge. Glue fabric to
outside, gluing excess to inside
edge. Cut fabric to fit inside mea-
surements of pieces exactly and
glue in place. Glue lace trim
along edges as shown in photograph. *To make buggy handles,*
cut two pieces of 18-gauge covered
wire to 9-inch lengths and wrap
each piece with florist's tape.
Hold both pieces of covered wire
together, grab ends with needle-
nosed pliers, and curl ends under
to form matching handles.

*Cut four wheels from card-
board,* using pattern as guide.
Paint wheels with acrylic paint.
Set aside to dry. Cut two pieces of
18-gauge covered wire approximately 5½ inches in length and
wrap with florist's tape. Slip one
wheel on each end of wire. Glue
in place to hold. Set aside to dry.

Cover outside edge of large
plastic foam base with ribbon,
gluing in place at 2-inch intervals. Glue ends down. Cut tulle

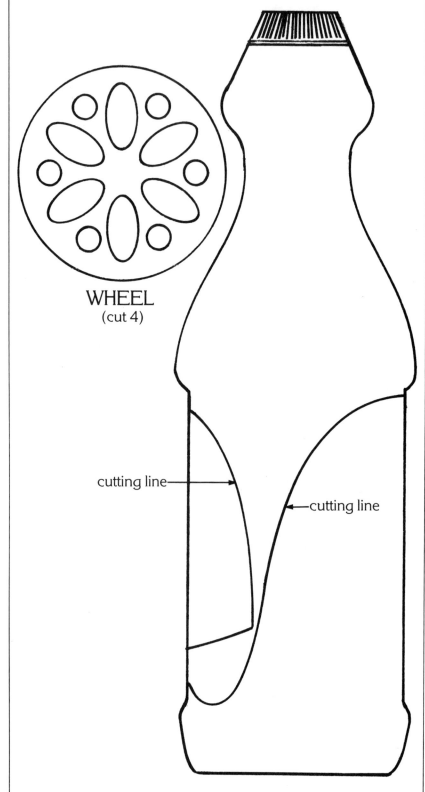

WHEEL
(cut 4)

cutting line

cutting line

148

into two 1½-yard pieces. Fold each piece in half lengthwise. Using a 12-inch length of 26-gauge wire as needle, gather double thickness of tulle on wire along fold. Fold ends of wire over to hold gathered tulle onto wire. Repeat with second 1½-yard piece. Attach wires and tulle along sides of large base, ½ inch from edges on both sides. Space and poke three toothpicks in middle of large base. Press small base on top to attach, letting tulle extend out underneath small base. Cut six pieces of ribbon to 18-inch lengths. Loop each ribbon three times and wire together at bottom. Stick ribbons into base at each corner and center sides. Set wheels onto middle of base and set buggy on wheel wires. Glue in place, if desired. Press handle wires into base at back of buggy as shown in photograph. Attach silk flowers and greenery to base and around base of buggy to fill in. Decorate inside of buggy with bows and silk flowers and greenery.

Wedding Announcement Birdhouse

This little bird is about to whisper something in your ear.

Materials:

1 round oatmeal box
1 paper towel tube
Brush-on or spray acrylic paint: white and blue
Fabric scraps
Eyelet lace and rickrack trimming
3 paper plates 12″ diameter
White tacky glue
Stapler (optional)
Spray glue
Fine diamond-dust glitter
Toilet tissue tube
4 moving eyes 10 mm.
White silk flowers
3″ dowel stick ¼″ diameter
2 yds. ⅝″-wide ribbon

Instructions:

Remove lid from box and cut top off so box is 6 inches high. Cut hole 2 inches in diameter in side of box approximately ½ inch up from bottom edge. Cut paper towel tube to 7 inches. Center end in bottom of the box and trace around tube. Cut hole in bottom, following guide line. Place lid back on box. Paint box and lid white (or cover box with fabric). Glue eyelet embroidery trim around bottom edge of box and glue rickrack around opening in side. *To make top of birdhouse,* cut a pie-shaped wedge from one paper plate. Overlap and glue or staple cut edges. Let dry. Spray top of house with spray glue and sprinkle with diamond-dust glitter. Place end of paper towel tube in middle of second paper plate and trace around tube. Cut hole in middle of paper plate following guide line. Spray paper towel tube with white spray paint or cover with fabric. *To assemble* *birdhouse,* insert 1½ inches of paper towel tube into bottom of oatmeal box. Glue in place to hold. Let dry completely. Next, turn whole paper plate with hole in center face down on table, and insert paper towel tube into hole. Glue tube to paper plate.

To make birds, cut four lengths of toilet tissue tube, ¾ inch each. Glue two pieces of tube together for each bird. Let dry. Paint tubes blue. Cut tails and beaks from middle of remaining paper plate, using pattern as guide. Paint pieces blue. Glue tails and beaks onto tubes. Glue eyes in place. *To* *make bird's hat,* cut a 1 inch x 3 inch strip and a circle 1½ inches in diameter from middle of remaining paper plate. Glue strip together, overlapping ends to form a tube. Glue tube to middle of circle. Glue hat to top of one bird's head. Glue silk flowers to top of other bird's head. Punch a small hole in side of oatmeal box ½ inch below opening in side. Insert dowel into hole and glue in place for perch. Glue bird with silk flowers onto perch and bird with hat onto paper plate. Decorate base and birdhouse with silk flowers and ribbon.

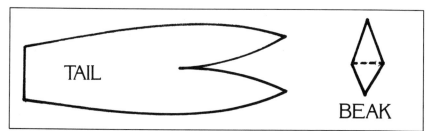

TAIL

BEAK

Money Tree

For the silver anniversary party, buy the numerals "25" to hang from the top. You'll have to tape them to covered wire bent in their shape, and then attach to the tree with more tape. Or cut the numerals from lightweight cardboard, glue foil to both sides with a piece of wire under the foil on one side for attaching to tree, and tape to tree.

Materials:

18-gauge covered wire: two 18″ lengths, four 12″ lengths, four 8″ lengths, three 6″ lengths, three 4″ lengths, two 2″ lengths
White florist's tape ½″ wide
Needle-nosed pliers
2 plastic foam discs, 1″ x 6″ and 1″ x 8″
White tacky glue
3 wooden toothpicks
3 yds. 1″ wide ribbon, made into 2 multi-looped bows, 5 loops each side (see instructions page 158)
1 yd. ⅛″ wide ribbon
White paper or metallic-foil 8″ doilies
About 21 bills for trim

Instructions:

To make tree: Wrap all lengths of covered wire with white florist's tape. Grab ends of all wires, except the two 18-inch lengths, with needle-nosed pliers and curl to form loops at one end. To start assembling the tree, hold the two 18-inch lengths side by side and start wrapping again with florist's tape. Approximately ½ inch down from the top, add one 2-inch length of wire by placing the straight end of wire against the double wire base and attaching to base by continuing to wrap with tape. Add the remainder of the branches in the same manner, in-

creasing length size as you work down the base. Bend branches for shape. *To make base,* stick three wooden toothpicks into middle of large plastic foam disc and press small disc on top. Attach doilies to base in desired pattern; glue in place. Attach tree to base by pressing wire into middle of base. Stick the two multi-looped bows into base at bottom of tree. Trim tree and base with small bows tied from ⅛-inch ribbon and bills that have been fan-folded.

Children's Party Clown

Materials:

Plastic foam ball 3″ diameter
Acrylic paint: black and flesh-color
Plastic foam base 1″ x 4″ x 10″
Plastic foam disc ¾″ x 5¾″
Fabric scraps to cover foam base and line flowers
Rickrack trim (optional)
White tacky glue
Plastic spoons: 12 each yellow, red, and orange
Wire cutters
Chenille stems: 2 each red, yellow, orange, blue, purple, and green; 6 white
30″ length ¼″ green plastic stem tubing, or green ½″ florist's tape
Art paper: light green and dark green
4 pieces 26-gauge wire, 12″ each
2 moving eyes 12 mm.
1 red wooden bead ¼″ diameter for nose
Felt scraps: red, blue, yellow, and pink
Pinking shears (optional)
2 white chenille bumps
Toilet tissue tube
Lightweight cardboard
Ribbon for bow tie (optional)

Instructions:

Paint foam ball flesh-color. Set aside to dry. Cover foam base and disc with fabric. Glue in place to hold. Glue disc to top of base. Glue rickrack trim to outside of bases, if desired. *To make flowers,* cut handles from spoons with wire cutters. Each flower uses six spoons. To start each flower, overlap two spoons halfway and glue in place to hold. Let set. Continue to add remaining petals, overlapping to form flower, gluing in place. Let set to dry. Make six flowers. *To attach flower to stem,* fold ½ inch of one end of white chenille stem. Insert chenille stem through top of flower and glue folded end of chenille stem to inside base of flower. Glue fabric scrap to inside of flower, if desired, to cover chenille stem end. Cut stems on two flowers to 6 inches, two to 5 inches, and remaining two to 4 inches. Cover chenille stems with plastic stem tube cut to fit with wire cutters or cover by taping. Cut six calyxes from dark green art paper, using pattern as guide. Glue in place to back of flower. Set aside to dry. Cut four leaves from light green art paper, using pattern as guide. Glue wire to back of each leaf. Set aside to dry.

To make clown, glue eyes in place on painted foam ball. Glue nose in place. Using pattern as guide, cut mouth from red felt and glue in place. Cut hat from red felt. Overlap and glue cut edges, to form cone shape. Glue hat to top of head. Cut strip of blue felt measuring ½ inch x 8 inches. One edge may be cut with pinking shears, if desired. Glue strip around edge of hat overlapping and gluing excess in back. Glue two chenille bumps below front rim of hat. *To make body,* insert the twelve remaining chenille stems into bottom of head, in a circle, alternating colors of stems. Insert other ends of chenille stems into middle of round base in a 1-inch diameter circle (see photograph). Press down on head to bend chenille stems into shape of clown's body as shown. *To make arms,* cut from blue felt, using pattern as guide. Gather cuff with basting stitch where indicated. Glue arms to body at neckline and side as shown in photograph. Cut two hands from yellow felt, using pattern as guide. Glue in place under cuffs. *To make collar,* cut pink felt strip 2 inches x 10 inches. Scallop one edge as shown in photograph. Gather collar along straight edge with basting stitch and tie around neck. Place plastic spoon flowers around side of clown, using photo as guide, by pressing chenille stems covered with tubing or wrapped with florist's tape into base. Press wires on leaves into base around flowers. *To make shoes,* cut a ¾-inch length of toilet tissue tube. Cut piece in half, to form two half circles. Cut a piece of cardboard to fit one side of each half circle and glue in place. Paint black. Let dry. Glue shoes to base at front of body. Glue ribbon bow tie to neck, if desired.

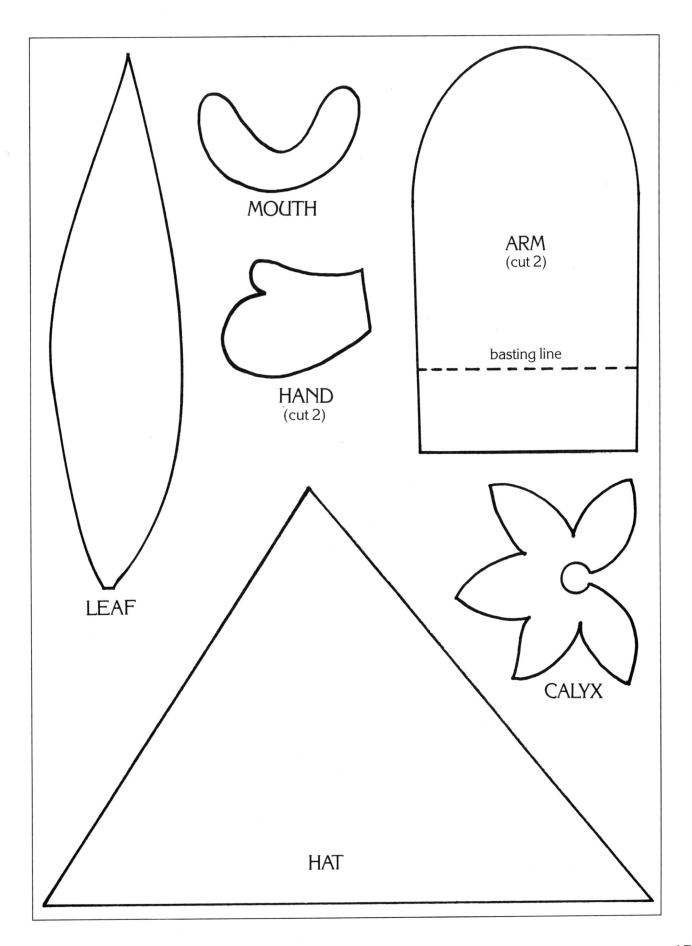

MOUTH

HAND
(cut 2)

ARM
(cut 2)

basting line

LEAF

CALYX

HAT

153

Three Wise Men: Free-Standing Sculpture

Materials (for one figure):

Velvet fabric for cape, hat, sleeves

Needle and thread

White tacky glue

Gold braid, rickrack, ribbon, etc., for trim

1 yd. yarn for hair and beard

1 bottle (quart liquor bottles make the best bases)

Compass for drawing crown

Assorted jewels, sequins, rhinestones, etc., for trim

Small wrapped box or square wooden bead, costume jewelry for gifts

Instructions:

Cut cape from velvet, using pattern as guide and shortening if necessary to fit bottle height. Turn raw edges under and hem to finish edge. Cut sleeves. Turn raw edges under and hem. Glue trim to edges, if desired. Glue yarn onto bottle top, starting at back for hair and bringing around to front for beard. Use photograph as guide for placement, zigzagging yarn back and forth for texture. Cut a 1½-inch piece of yarn for mustache and glue in place. *To make crown,* cut 3-inch diameter circle from fabric. Glue circle to top of bottle, gathering and overlapping to fit rim. Glue trim around raw edge of cap to finish. Glue sleeves in place on sides of bottle. Glue cape in place at neckline. Using photograph as guide or creating your own design, trim with various jewels, braids, etc. Glue gifts ("gold," "frankincense," and "myrrh") to front of each wise man and glue ends of sleeves to gifts as shown in photo.

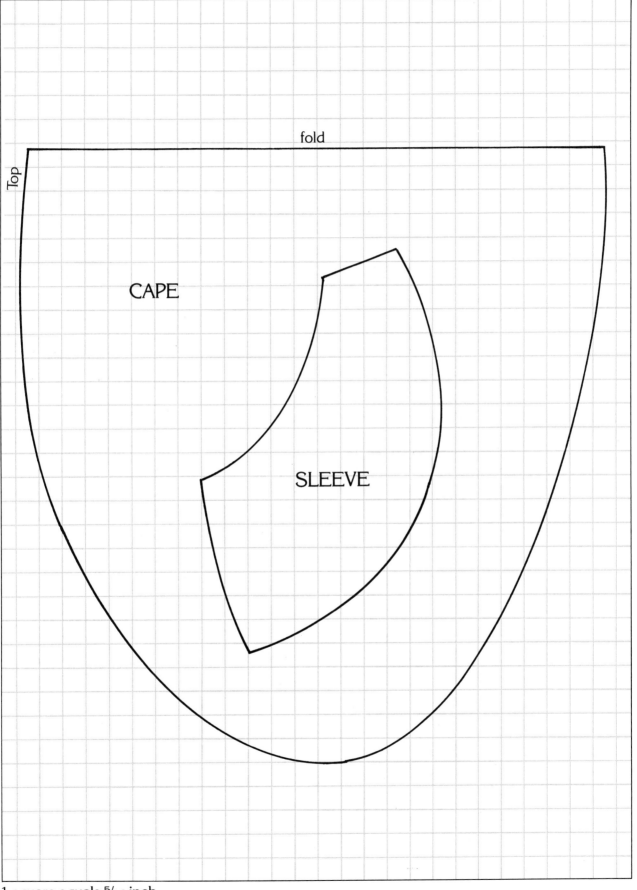

fold

Top

CAPE

SLEEVE

1 square equals 5/16 inch

How-To's of Pinecone Clusters, Multi-Looped Bows, and Ribbon Roses

How to Make a Pinecone Cluster with Trim

Especially at Christmas, craft and florist shops sell prewired miniature cones and berries ready to be made into clusters. They also sell the premade clusters.

Materials:

5 or 6 miniature cleaned dried pinecones (see page 8) approx. 1″ long
6 or 7 pieces 26-gauge wire, about 3″ or 4″ each
Artificial red berries
Florist's tape ½″ wide

Instructions:

To make a stem for your pinecones, wrap a piece of wire around the bottom row of scales on each cone. Pull the wire very tight around the cone and bring the wire ends together. The red artificial berries are generally available double-ended with string stems. These stems need to be strengthened to be added to cluster. Fold stems in half so that berries are together, then wrap a wire tightly around the base of the berries.

Holding five or six pinecones in your hand and three or four berry clusters, wrap the stems together with florist's tape. To do this, lay the tape alongside the stem and twirl the wire, *stretching* the tape and guiding it on a slight diagonal down the stem until the wire is covered. Be sure to stretch the tape so that the stem remains as thin as possible. Cut the cluster stem to desired length before inserting into the foam wreath or base.

Note: Plain wire will not hold in foam, but needs to be wrapped with tape before being inserted.

How to Tie a Multi-Looped Bow

Instructions:

Hold the ribbon in your right hand, dull side toward you, leaving a tail to the top of about 3 inches, Fig. 1. Loop the short end down and around the thumb, Fig. 2. The wrong side of the satin will face you, so twist the ribbon at the back of the thumb to bring the satin side out, Fig. 3. Make this twist exactly in the center of your thumb and make a very definite twist. Now your center loop and two ends are satin-side-out. *You should be holding the ribbon in your right hand with thumb in front and your index and middle finger in the back.*

Make a small loop to the bottom, 1 inch long. Catch this loop with your middle finger, Fig. 4. Twist to get satin side out. Repeat with a loop to the top. Catch this loop with your index finger. Twist again to get the satin side out. *Always make your loops to the back, then twist to bring the satin side out.* Now a third loop to the bottom, twist, and a fourth loop to the top and twist, Fig. 5. Loops will be approximately 2 inches long. The small loops in the center are for fluffiness, the two longer loops determine the size of your bow. The bow should be 4 to 6 inches overall.

Each time you make a loop, twist to bring the satin side out. Be sure that the twist comes in the same place each time. This twist will enable you to place your loop where you want. Instead of building your bow with one loop under the other, as shown in Fig. 6, you build loops to either side as shown in Fig. 7. *Always alternate a loop to the top, a loop to the bottom.*

When you have a bow of the desired size, change the bow over to your left hand and place a wire through the center loop as shown in Fig. 8. Work the wire around to the back and, holding the loops up in a bunch (Fig. 9), give the wires at the back a twist and tighten as much as possible. Use a pair of pliers, if necessary. This wiring ensures the success of your bow. If the wire is tight, you will be able to pull the loops around and arrange them in an artistic manner, making a very full circular bow. The loops will stay in place as shown in Fig. 10. Wiring also enables you to attach the bow to your design.

Note: These instructions are specifically for satin ribbon; however, any type of ribbon can be substituted. The length of ribbon used depends on the size of the bow desired. Any width of ribbon is fine.

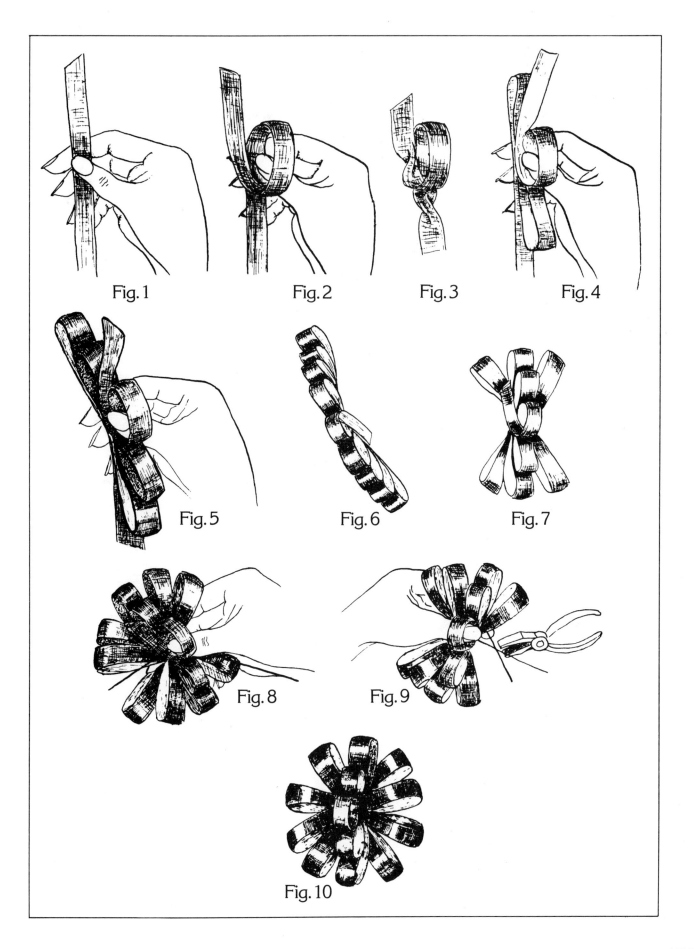

Fig. 1

Fig. 2

Fig. 3

Fig. 4

Fig. 5

Fig. 6

Fig. 7

Fig. 8

Fig. 9

Fig. 10

How to Make a Ribbon Floribunda Rose

Instructions:

To make a rose, use one yard of ribbon and hold with the wrong side facing you. Fold end of ribbon down toward you, Fig. 1, then fold over as shown in Fig. 2. Roll this end straight across to within ½ inch of end and top fold. Arrow in Fig. 2 shows where to stop rolling. Wrap a wire around roll, 1 inch down from top to form stem. Be sure to catch some of bottom edge of ribbon so it will not unroll. Roll bud and fold ribbon back, laying it flat against stem, Fig. 3. Each time you turn the rose, fold ribbon back so bottom edge is again against stem, Fig. 4. This shows top view of rose. Shaded areas are the wrong side of ribbon. Fold and turn as you work, holding rose flat between fingers of your right hand. When ribbon is used up, fasten end to stem with a piece of wire. The rose will have four or five layers of ribbon. Tape an 18-gauge wire to the stem if needed, and add artificial rose leaves if desired.

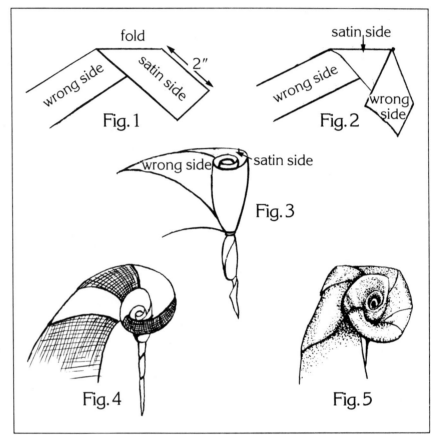

Material Matters: Notes on Materials, Methods, and Sources

One of the most satisfying aspects of scrap-crafting is that it requires practically no special equipment, few technical skills, and almost nothing in bulk that you cannot find in your own home or outdoors, free for the taking. The materials you do need are widely available through chain five-and-tens, craft and hobby shops, notions departments of department stores, and through craft mail-order catalogs like *Lee Ward's*, (1200 St. Charles, Elgin, IL 61020), *Craft Source* (9121 E. Las Lunas Drive, Box 68, Temple City, CA 91780), *Cole National* (5885 Grant Ave., Cleveland, OH 44105), and *American Handicrafts* (801 Foch St., Fort Worth, TX 76107).

Antiquing materials. Gold or metallic pastes like Rub'n Buff or Treasure Gold give a gilded, antique-like finish when applied according to manufacturer's directions. Both products are nationally available through craft stores.

Another antiquing method, described in the Antiqued Plant Containers from Paper project (page 28), uses brown paint (any other dark paint will do) applied to a lighter painted surface, then wiped off immediately so that the dark color remains only in the sunken parts of the design. Follow the caution note and test the compatibility of the two paints. Seal when dry.

Basic equipment. We assume that you already have most of the following tools around the house; they are not listed in individual projects:

pencil and paper; ruler and tape measure; embroidery and sewing needles with thread; sharp scissors; stapler; heavy-duty wire cutter (which we do list, in case you have to bring it in from the garage or wherever you store garden supplies); straight pins; corsage pins; small, inexpensive paint brushes; cotton swabs and small sticks for applying glue and paint.

Cardboard. You should be saving shirt cardboards, and wrapping and binding materials in this category. Cut with heavy scissors or sharp knife as needed.

Corrugated cardboard in sheet form or cut from boxes is also useful. Tear or cut the cartons apart with a sharp knife or wire cutters. Bend flattened board back parallel to its fluting and cut to desired size and shape with a sharp knife. To use the board at right angles to the fluting, measure it first, then score along measured line by cutting partway through with a sharp knife, single-edge razor blade, or X-acto knife. Bend the board back, then cut it all the way through. If the edges or layers fray or separate, tape them closed.

Chenille stems and bumps. The stems, really upgraded pipe cleaners, are now more widely available than the cleaners. You can find them, and the bumps, at craft and hobby shops.

Florist's tape (floral tape). Sold in rolls ½ inch and 1 inch wide, green, brown, or white, at craft and hobby shops and florist-supply centers. See page 18 for valuable hints on using it.

Glaze or varnish. Either one is a good finisher or sealer, giving a smooth, transparent coating to the design. Decoupeurs and furniture finishers have some preference for clear varnish, so this is the finish to use for flat paper surfaces and wood. But glaze is less expensive and can be used for most projects. Matte or gloss finish? We specify when we have a preference. Spray or brush-on? Again, a personal choice. No brush to clean when you spray, but you must keep the holes free, and work carefully to avoid build-up of too much glaze where spray circles overlap. Joli brush-on glaze and Accent spray glaze are well-known brands at craft and hobby shops.

When applying either glaze or varnish, follow manufacturer's directions; work in a well-ventilated area away from open flame. Test the compatability of the glaze or varnish to the background by applying it first to a small hidden area, just as you do paint. If it buckles or lifts the base coat, you'll have to try some other brand or type of sealer. Be sure that you let the finish dry thoroughly before use. Time varies: instant drying glazes and varnishes have been market-tested and sold in some areas.

Glues. You'll need these different types:

Clear glue, which is translucent when dry, especially for holding imbedded stones in jewelry projects and for tissue paper designs or where you want glue to penetrate. Apply with a very soft brush. Snow Foam, Pactra Clear Glue, or Bond 727 are well-known brands.

Spray-on glue provides a clean, simple way to apply glitter or sparkle.

Hot glue, which is fast-drying and holds heavy materials like shells or pinecones in place. Sold in cakes to be melted in a pan, or in a cylinder that fits into a special glue gun. Follow package directions when using this flammable material.

White tacky glue, which is thick with solids and was developed as an all-purpose craft glue. It is clear and flexible when dry, so materials never pop off the background to which they are applied. Spread on with fingers, toothpick, piece of twig, Popsicle stick, or with an inexpensive brush. Three major brands are on the market in craft shops nationwide—Aleene's (developed by the author), Wilhold, and Bond.

Jewelry findings. Mountings for pendants and earrings, pin backs, jump rings for necklaces, chains, silver tube for crimping line, beads and rings, moving eyes, etc. Salvage them from discarded jewelry, purchase from local hobby and craft shops, or see under this heading in telephone book yellow pages.

Paint. Acrylic paints are water soluble, washable (clean-up is easy), fast-drying, odorless, and available in many colors. Choose spray-on—perhaps easier to apply on an ornamented surface —or apply with an inexpensive brush, following manufacturer's directions.

Some guidelines: Always test paint on a small hidden area before you apply it generally. A second coat of paint applied over another color or brand of paint may cause a first coat to lift or buckle, which means the two paints are incompatible. If so, you'll have to try another brand or type. A particular brand may not be available everywhere, so we cannot make brand recommendations. However, Krylon, Snow Foam, and Accent have wide distribution in the craft field.

Paper. Probably no material is more abundant in modern households than paper, and to be truly economical, you need buy none at all. Just salvage colorfully printed or plain covers, fine department-store bags, wrapping papers, and similar materials to use in scrap-craft projects. But should you elect to buy some of the papers called for, there are important distinctions between art paper and construction paper. Nevertheless, they can be used interchangeably for different results.

Art paper, specified in most of the projects in chapter 2, is smooth and hard and sized to hold its shape (like starched fabric). It takes colors well, and resists fading. You can buy it in pads or in sheets, and in many different weights, thicknesses, sizes, and finishes.

Construction paper, considerably less expensive, is blotter-like. It tears, frays, and fades easily. It is available usually fifty sheets to a package, in size 9″ x 12″ or larger.

Pinecones and other dried natural materials are abundant in nature, but if you are not able to pick them up free and dry following instructions on page 8, you can order them from Nature's Harvest, 3356 Motor Avenue, Los Angeles, CA 90034.

Plastic foam. You can buy it in hobby, craft, and notions stores everywhere, in balls, blocks, discs, eggs, rings, and wreaths. Cut it with a sharp knife, a single-edge razor blade, or an electric hot wire cutter. (Styrofoam is a brand name for this product.)

"Popsicle" sticks. If you can't collect enough left-over sticks, you can buy them at many craft and hobby stores. Or send for them from Forster Manufacturing, Wilton, ME 04294, or Solon Mfg. Co., Ferry Street, Solon, ME 04979. The sticks can be cut with wire cutters, a knife, or a small saw if you wish to use one.

Shells. If local beaches or local shops can't provide them, order by mail from Florida Supply House, Inc., Box 847, Bradenton, FL 33506, or Sea Shells Int., 340 Barneveld Ave., San Francisco, CA 94124.

Trimmings. No scrap-crafter has to be told to save the ribbons, bows, tiny artificial flowers, remnants of lace, braid, rickrack, eyelet lace, satin cording, sequin and gold chenille glitter, and felt and fabric remnants for cut outs and appliqués. Dozens of trimmings of all kinds come in with gift packages. Techniques for making special trimmings like ribbon roses and multi-looped bows are described on pages 160 and 158.

Wire. Even wire accumulates as scrap if you save the twists packed with plastic bags. For longer pieces, you will have to get to a craft, hobby, or notions store (or wherever florist's materials are sold). Remember that the higher the gauge, the finer the wire. For making stems on flowers, use 18-gauge wire; 22-gauge is for use with medium-weight projects; 26-gauge for light wiring jobs. Wire should be cut with wire cutters. It is sold bare or wrapped, in sticks in 12-inch or 18-inch lengths. Also sold in coils, rolls, and on spools (good for making garlands or any project requiring continuous wiring over a relatively large surface).

Index

Make your home special

Since 1922, millions of men and women have turned to *Better Homes and Gardens* magazine for help in making their homes more enjoyable places to be. You, too, can trust *Better Homes and Gardens* to provide you with the best in ideas, inspiration and information for better family living.

In every issue you'll find ideas on food and recipes, decorating and furnishings, crafts and hobbies, remodeling and building, gardening and outdoor living plus family money management, health, education, pets, car maintenance and more.

For information on how you can have *Better Homes and Gardens* delivered to your door, write to: Mr. Robert Austin, P.O. Box 4536, Des Moines, IA 50336.

Better Homes and Gardens ®

*The Idea Magazine
for Better Homes
and Families*